Septuagint: Wisdom of Joshua ben Sira and Odes

Septuagint, Volume 18

SCRIPTURAL RESEARCH INSTITUTE

Published by Digital Ink Productions, 2024

Copyright

Septuagint: Wisdom of Joshua ben Sira and Odes

Second edition. December 23, 2024

Copyright © 2024 Scriptural Research Institute.

ISBN: 978-1-998636-13-6

The Wisdom of Joshua ben Sira was written by Joshua ben Sira ben Eleazar in Aramaic circa 200 BC. The Greek translation was made in Alexandria by Joshua's grandson in 132 BC.

The Book of Odes was added to the Septuagint in the early Christian era, and is mostly a collection of older songs and prayers found in the Septuagint, however, it was not made from the Septuagint's translations, but from Theodotion's translation of circa 200 AD.

This English translation was created by the Scriptural Research Institute in 2020 through 2024, primarily from the Codex Sinaiticus and Codex Alexandrinus. Additionally, the Genizah manuscripts of the Wisdom of Joshua ben Sira were used for comparative analysis, and the Aleppo Codex, Leningrad Codex, and Dead Sea Scrolls have been used for comparison of parallel verses found in the Book of Odes.

The image used for the cover is an artistic reinterpretation of "Elijah Taken Up in a Chariot of Fire," painted by Giuseppe Angeli between 1740 and 1755.

Table of Contents

TABLE OF CONTENTS

TABLE OF CONTENTS

TABLE OF CONTENTS

Forward

After the death of Alexander the Great in 323 BC, his generals ripped apart his empire, and by 305 BC General Ptolemy had gained control of the Eastern Mediterranean, including Egypt, Judea, Cyprus, Cyrene, and coastal regions of modern Turkey, including Cilicia, Pamphylia, Lycia, and Caria. He established the dynasty of the Ptolemys that would rule Egypt for the next three centuries until Cleopatra VII Philopator committed suicide in 30 BC. The Ptolemys built one of the great wonders of the ancient world, the Library of Alexandria, which at its height was said to house over 400,000 scrolls. The original collection that was amassed in the first century of the library, was largely Greek works, and translations of Egyptian works, however in the mid-3rd century BC, King Ptolemy II Philadelphus ordered a translation of the ancient Israelite scriptures for the library.

A number of Judahite and Samaritan scholars were assembled, numbering either 70 or 72 depending on the version of the story, and representing every Israelite sect. They created a translation of the ancient Israelite scriptures later known as the Septuagint. The early collections of Israelite texts translated included the Torah, the Dodeka, and the books of Enoch, however, by the mid-2nd century BC, most of the Septuagint had been translated. The Wisdom of Joshua ben Sira was an independently translated early Jewish collection of wisdom proverbs translated in 132 BC according to the prologue by the author. The translator claimed to be the grandson of Joshua ben Sira, who had moved to Egypt, and found that there were no books of minor wisdom among the Septuagint, so translated his grandfather's collection. A second collection called Odes was added as an appendix in the early Christian era.

The Book of Joshua ben Sira is known by several names, including Sirach, the Wisdom of Sirach, the Wisdom of Jesus Sirach ben Sira, Ecclesiasticus, and the Book of the All-Virtuous Wisdom of Yeshua ben Sira. This diversity of names is based on the fact that the Masoretes did not copy the text, however, an Aramaic copy and some fragments of the ancient Hebrew version have survived. The conflicting names of Yehoshua ben Sira, used in Hebrew translations, and variations of Jesus Sirach, used in Christian translations, are derived from the Hebrew and Greek variants of his name. This translation uses the name of Joshua ben Sira, translated from the Judeo-Aramaic name Yšûô bn Syrå (ישוע בן סירא), as that appears to be the oldest variant.

There is a great deal of debate about who the translator and original author were, and some Jewish scholars have suggested the book was not written in Jerusalem, but in Egypt. The debates regarding who these people were are largely based on the Hebrew translations of the book, which all appear to have been done after the Greek translation. The translator does refer to the original work of his grandfather as having been in Ebraesti (Εβραιστὶ), which is the modern Greek word for Hebrew, however, at the time, Hebrew was a "new" language, and the term was being used for both Aramaic and Hebrew.

Hebrew was a newly reformed and standard language developed and promoted by the Hasmonean Dynasty which had gained control of Judea in 140 BC. It was based on the ancient dialect of Canaanite spoken in the region, however, used the Aramaic script instead of the traditional Phoenician script. The name Hebrew was based on the patriarch Eber from the Torah, who was an ancestor of not just the Judahites and Israelites, like Jacob, and Edomites, like Abraham, but almost all Western Semitic peoples. The Hasmonean Dynasty appears to have been trying to create a literary language that could compete with Greek, and unite the peoples of Judea, Phoenicia, and Syria. The ancient texts were translated into this new language from Aramaic and Phoenician (Judahite, Samaritan, and Edomite), and standardized versions of the texts were created. According to the books of Maccabees, the Hasmonean Dynasty paid for scribes to translate the ancient texts that people brought to them and provided copies in the new language.

Unfortunately, very few people could read this language, and a division developed between the Sadducees, the ruling group of priests and religious lawyers, and the Aramaic-speaking people of Judea. When General Pompey overthrew the Hasmonean Dynasty in 69 BC and passed Judea to Herod, the King of Edom, a new group of Aramaic translations began to circulate in Judea known as the Targum, which was partially based on the Hebrew translation and partially based on the Septuagint. This reinforced the idea that the Hebrew text was older, an idea that continued to grow through the Classical Era, especially after the split between Christians, who mostly spoke Greek and Aramaic, and the Jews, who wanted nothing to do with them, and so embraced the Hebrew language as part of their identity.

The concept that Hebrew was the "original" language developed within Jewish thought. The early Medieval era Midrash, a collection of Jewish interpretations of biblical passages, reported that Adam must have spoken Hebrew as he gave his wife a Hebrew name, Ḥŭh (חוה), which only makes sense in Hebrew. Naturally, this interpretation was based on the Hebrew translation of Bereshít, the Masoretic version of Cosmic Genesis, and would have resulted in the conclusion that Adam must have spoken Greek if it was based on the Septuagint, as

Adam named his wife Zoe (Ζωή) in the Septuagint's Cosmic Genesis. The Syriac-speaking Christians of the era claimed her original name in the Aramaic version of Genesis was Ḥůå (**חוה**), which they rendered as Ḥaůå (ܚܘܐ) in Syriac.

Nevertheless, while some Medieval Jewish scholars accepted the idea that Hebrew was the original language, most seem to have rejected the idea. Conversely, the idea gained acceptance in both the Islamic and Christian nations. The 13th century Islamic historian Abu al-Fida theorized that Hebrew was named after the patriarch Eber because he refused to help with the building of the Tower of Babel, and so he retained the original language. It is worth noting that Islamic sources at the time believed that all Arabic peoples were descended from Eber, and so the "original Hebrew language" would have been a form of Arabic. In European countries, the idea that Hebrew was the original "Adamic" language became deeply entrenched in Christian thought, so much so, that many Christians still believe it.

Archaeologically speaking, Hebrew cannot be traced back to before the Maccabean Revolt, which led to the Hasmonean Dynasty. It probably formed because many urban Jews that knew Aramaic had fled Jerusalem, and were living among rural Jews that spoke the older dialect of the region. The revolt lasted 25 years, and so an entire generation grew up as the Judeans struggled for independence from the rule of the Greeks. Simon the Zealot, the first King/High Priest of the Hasmonean Dynasty, who took the throne in 140 BC, was clearly politically motivated and sent ambassadors to Rome to explain that the Jews were Romans, and they worshiped Jupiter Sabazius, but the Jews were doing it the correct way, and the Romans should follow their lead. He sent a similar message to the Spartans according to the books of Maccabees. The Romans did not respond well to this, as recorded by Valerius Maximus:

> "Gnaeus Cornelius Hispalus, praetor peregrinus in the year of the consulate of Marcus Popilius Laenas and Lucius Calpurnius, ordered the astrologers by an edict to leave Rome and Italy within ten days, since by a fallacious inter-pretation of the stars they perturbed fickle and silly minds, thereby making profit out of their lies. The same praetor compelled the Jews, who attempted to infect the Roman custom with the cult of Jupiter Sabazius, to return to their homes."

As the Maccabean Revolt had raged against Greek rule in Judea, between 165 and 140 BC, the Romans were fighting the final, and bloodiest of their wars against the Carthaginians, the ancient Canaanite colony based in modern Tunisia. The Carthaginians were once the great power of the Western Mediterranean, domi-nating northwest Africa, southern and western Iberia,

Sicily, Sardinia, and Corsica. The Romans had been at almost constant war against Carthage for over a century, beginning with the first Punic war in 264 BC, and in 146 BC finally defeated them, and effectively exterminated the race. Roman records report that they forced the surviving Carthaginian warriors to fight to the death in arenas, while the civilians were sold as slaves to anyone who would buy them. The population of northwest Africa became a slave race for centuries and was not freed until the rise of Christianity in the 4th century.

Carthage had been the last independent power to write in the old Phoenician script, although some smaller nations like Edom were still using it. The choice to switch to the Aramaic script, which made the new official language of Judea more accessible to most Semitic-speaking peoples in Syria, Phoenicia, and Mesopotamia, was probably another political decision by Simon, however, it did not result in wide acceptance, and in most respects, this linguistic reform was a failure.

While Hebrew did replace Aramaic and Phoenician as the religious language of some Jewish sects, it increased the division between the Jews and Samaritans, as the Samaritans refused to switch scripts, and also created a division between the Jews and Aramaic speaking Israelite groups, which ultimately formed the core of the early Christian communities. Hebrew was rarely used for anything other than religious studies throughout Jewish history, and virtually all important Jewish literature produced in the Middle East was written in Aramaic, including both versions of the Talmud. In Europe, two Yiddish languages developed, one based on Germanic, and one based on Slavic, and almost all European Jewish literature was written in these two languages. Until the State of Israel was created, 2088 years after the Kingdom of Judea gained independence, Hebrew had been a failed language. Israel used Hebrew as an official language, and banned Yiddish, creating the first state in which Hebrew was used as the common language.

Hebrew and Aramaic fragments of the Wisdom of Joshua ben Sira were in circulation during the Herodian Dynasty, and fragments have survived among the Dead Sea Scrolls, including the 2QSir, 11QPs[a], and MasSir scrolls, however, the fragments may not have been part of a book called the Wisdom of Joshua Ben Sira. The 2QSir and MasSir scrolls are so damaged that they are barely recognizable as being excerpts from Joshua ben Sira, and the Great Psalms Scroll, while being one of the best-preserved scrolls found in the Qumran caves, includes random psalms and proverbs from multiple sources, including excerpts that may be from Joshua ben Sira. As the Wisdom of Joshua ben Sira was itself a collection of proverbs that Joshua had collected, these scrolls may have simply drawn on the same sources.

The text in the Great Psalms Scroll that might be drawn from the Wisdom of Joshua ben Sira is from chapter 51, however, all the surviving verses are much shorter, and all references to "God," the "Lord," and "Yhůh" are missing. This could not have been done by the scribe that compiled the scroll, as the name Yhůh (𐤉𐤄𐤅𐤄) spelled in the Phonician way is used in the ortherwise Hebrew text of the scroll. The scribe clearly did not have a problem using the name, which indicates that either the name was not in his source text, or he removed a different name that was.

One possibility indicated within the Greek translation is that the original text included references to Bôl Ḥmm (𐤁𐤏𐤋 𐤇𐤌𐤌), generally anglicized as Lord Hammon, the supreme god of the Carthaginians at the time. Lord Hammon was commonly referred to Bôl (𐤁𐤏𐤋), meaning "Lord" and Mlk (𐤌𐤋𐤊), meaning "King," terms that often appear in the Greek and Latin translations of Judean texts from between 200 and 100 BC. Based on Roman records, and archeological evidence, the Carthaginians committed human sacrifice, which suggests it was a continuation of the cult of Moloch (Μολόχ) / Můlk (מולך) which was banned in Judah by King Josiah circa 625 BC. The Carthaginians considered Lord Hammon to be the same god as the Egyptian Amen (𓇋𓏠𓈖), Kushite Amanai (𐦀𐦉𐦐𐦃), and Meroitic Amni (𐦀𐦉𐦐). King Josiah's father, King Amon (אָמוֹן), was born when the Kushite Empire was still a major power, occupying Egypt, and challenging Assyria to the north of Judah. However, Kush was defeated by the Assyrians when Amon was very young, and the Kushites never regained control of Egypt. After King Amon's death, Josiah purged Judah of all gods other than Yhŭh. Lord Hammon was also known by the title Ba'al Qarnim (𐤁𐤏𐤋 𐤒𐤓𐤍𐤌), meaning "Lord Horns" or "Lord Radiance" which mirrors the description of god found in the Psalms, supporting Lord Hammon having once been a god worshipped in Judah.

Parallel verses to the Wisdom of Joshua ben Sira are found in the Talmud, a medieval era Jewish collection of laws and customs, which are accepted as paraphrases of Joshua ben Sira, however, he is never credited in the Talmud. Again, it is possible that the sources the rabbis used when compiling the Talmud were not Joshua ben Sira, but his sources. As his book does not appear to have been considered important to the Hasmonean Dynasty, and there does not appear to have been an official Hebrew translation, the Masoretes, a group of late Classical Era scribes did not copy the book, and only its Greek translation and translations based on the Greek were commonly available until the 1900s. In 1896, six medieval manuscripts of Hebrew translations of the Wisdom of Joshua ben Sira were discovered in the Cairo Genizah, a Jewish "cemetery of books." According to Jewish custom, worn-out Hebrew language texts are to be burned, and are stored in a room called a Genizah until the ceremonial burning, however, translations into other languages may be stored indefinitely.

The Cairo Genizah amassed over 400,000 worn-out copies of Jewish sacred literature over a thousand years, from 870 until the late 1800s when the collection was made available for academic study. Among these texts were six Hebrew translations of the Wisdom of Joshua ben Sira, which were never burned. The manuscripts date to the 10th through 12th centuries but do not survive intact. It is estimated that approximately two-thirds of the content found in the Greek translation survives among the Hebrew manuscripts, however, they do not match the Greek exactly, or each other.

One example of the differences between the Septuagint and Genizah manuscripts is in regards to where the name Yhů (יהʸ) must have been in Joshua's original work. The Septuagint's version of the book uses the term Cyriou (Κυρίου), which translates as "Lord," however, uses it inconsistently, sometimes as a title and sometimes as a name. Modern Greek translations render it as "Lord" (Κυρίου) and "the lord" (τὸν κύριον). Genizah manuscript

B uses the term yyy (״״), a medieval Jewish substitute for the name Yhůh, which was not to be copied except in the Masoretic texts. Genizah manuscript F contains an alternate substitute of ål (אל), meaning "god." According to the Talmud, the prohibition on using the name(s) of God(s), was introduced during the late Hasmonean Dynasty, likely to stop Jews from arguing about which God was the Jewish god.

As the original Greek translation was made before this, and the translator did use the term "god" (θεὸσ) in other places, there is no reason to believe he substituted the word "god" with "lord," or that he substituted the name Yhů with "lord" as a later Jewish translator would have done. The name Yhů was translated into Greek as Iaô (Ιαω) in other books of the Septuagint, as demonstrated by the Dead Sea Scroll Septuagint fragment 4QpapLXXLev[b], which dates from the Hasmonean Dynasty. In the early centuries of Christianity, the Christians and Gnostics debated the nature of Yhů, some interpreting him as God, and others as the devil, and eventually, the name was removed from the Septuagint. As a result, while it is found in some early fragments of the Septuagint, it is not found in any of the surviving Greek translations of the Wisdom of Joshua ben Sira.

Archaeological evidence shows that Yhů and his wife Anat were popular Israelite gods in the Persian era, however, it appears as if only Yhǔ was worshiped at the temples that Zerubbabel and Ezra built in Jerusalem. During the Greek era, Dionysus, known in Aramaic as Lord Sabaoth appears to have supplanted Yhǔ until the Hasmonean Dynasty restored Yhǔ in the form of Yhǔh. The fact that Genizah manuscript B uses the term yyy (""") where the Septuagint used the word "Lord" as a name supports the name Yhǔ as having been in the original collection by Joshua, as no scribe would have both added and redacted the banned name. Therefore, the name is restored in this translation in the earliest Latin transliteration of Iaw.

The pronunciation and therefore spelling of the name has always been debated, which is likely why the Hasmonean King/High Priests banned the name from general use and was a contributing factor to the Christians removing the name from their scriptures. According to Origen of Alexandria in the late 2nd century AD the Phoenician variant of Yhǔh (𐤀𐤄𐤅𐤆), which he referred to as the "most ancient script," was the most accurate. According to Theodoret of Cyprus in the 5th century, Samaritans pronounced the name as Yabe (Ιαβε) or Yabai (Ιαβαι). In the 1300s BC, a Canaanite god named Yǔ (𒅀𒉿) was mentioned in the Ugaritic Texts but does not appear to have been popular in northern Canaan, as little was recorded of him.

As Aaron, the first cohen of Yhůh, was a priest in the Egyptian city of Ĩůnů (𓉺𓊖) before the Exodus, the name almost certainly originates with the north Egyptian word for the moon, Ĩôḥ (☽), which when treated as the name of the lunar god in Iunu was modified to Ĩôhů (𓂋𓈖𓇳𓂝), commonly transliterated as Iahw. Like the early depictions of Yhůh in Samaria, Iahw was depicted as being a calf, which Aaron is reported to have built a statue of shortly after the Israelites left Egypt.

The collection of proverbs Joshua amassed appears to date to many periods in Israelite history, and one proverb even appears to derive from the Wisdom of Amenemope, a text that originated in the Egyptian New Kingdom era, a millennium earlier. As the Wisdom of Amenemope appears to have been lost in Egypt by the Persian era, Joshua could not have quoted it directly. The Wisdom of Amenemope was rediscovered by Egyptologists in 1888, after being lost for around 2400 years. Subsequently, eight partial copies have been found, ranging in estimated dates of between 1069 and 500 BC. Several Egyptologists noted similarities between Proverbs and the Wisdom of Amenemope, culminating in Adolf Erman's 1924 paper that compared the two texts, and pointed out that the confusing verse in the Masoretic version of Proverbs 22: הֲלֹא כָתַבְתִּי לְךָ [שִׁלְשׁוֹם] כ] (שָׁלִישִׁים ק) בְּמוֹעֵצֹת וָדָעַת is very similar to a verse in chapter 30 of Wisdom of Amenemope, and the Hebrew verse makes more sense if the Hebrew text had a translation error. This error is now accepted by most major Christian denominations, and has resulted in Bibles from the late 20th century onward having the verse "Have I not written for you thirty sayings of counsel and knowledge," instead of "Have not I written to thee excellent things in counsel and knowledge," which was found in the King James Version.

Both Proverbs and the Wisdom of Joshua ben Sira were once declared heretical by a group of Jewish leaders, as recorded in the Talmud, Shabbat 30b, meaning that they were always seen as being similar, and also different in some way from the rest of the sacred Israelite scriptures. While Proverbs was ultimately canonized by the Hasmonean Dynasty the Wisdom of Joshua ben Sira appears to have simply faded from use. This debate regarding the heretical nature of the texts is not dated, however, had to have been sometime after Joshua published his collection, and the Hasmoneans canonized Proverbs, roughly between 185 and 135 BC.

Due to the range of the content, and the constantly fluctuating theology in Jerusalem under Persian and Greek rule, the proverbs that Joshua ben Sira are not consistent in their theology. Several gods or spirits are mentioned, including most prominently: Sophia (Σοφία), generally translated as Wisdom. Like Proverbs, in which she is mentioned extensively, and the Wisdom of Solomon, where the first half of the book is about her, she is given a supreme position in the Wisdom of Joshua ben Sira. The book begins with the statement: "Sophia comes from Iaw, and is with him forever." A couple of sentences later, the text reads, "Before everything, Sophia was created..." This certainly indicates that when the text was written, Sophia was considered second only to Iaw, a minor goddess within early Judaism if ever there was one, and it is not a wonder that the book was declared heretical by enough Jewish religious leaders to warrant being mentioned in the Talmud. As such, she mirrors the Voice of God found in first Maccabees, and the Word of God in the Christian Gospel of John. Both the Voice and the Word were recorded as being the first creation of god, indicating the Voice, Word, and Wisdom were all reinterpretations of the same basic concept.

The Greek name Sophia (Σοφία) is a Greek translation, and the Masoretic texts use the name Chachamot (חָכְמוֹת), a feminine plural indefinite form of chacham (חָכָם), meaning "wise" or "smart." The Aramaic word hkm (תֹעֲלֹ) likewise meant "to be wise," however, the plural infinite implies the meaning "wisdom," and the feminine form implies a goddess of wisdom. Given that the author of the Wisdom of Solomon described Sophia leading the Israelites out of Egypt, and seemed to be at odds with the Torah over the Israelites worshiping serpents, a clear reference to Moses' bronze serpent statue, it suggests that Sophia / Chachamot was originally the goddess that Miriam was the prophetess of, as she was clearly not the prophetess of Moses' god, which he himself clarified in the Torah when he inflicted Miriam with leprosy for speaking out against Moses, who he referred to as his "servant," a term meaning "prophet" in the context of the verse.

While Joshua's collection of proverbs may have included verses regarding Sophia / Chachamot, the core of the work is focused on revering Iaw, a name which he appeared to use interchangeably with the term "Lord," confirming that he did view Iaw as being the Lord of the temple in Jerusalem. This itself also seems to be confirmed by the differences between the Septuagint and Genizah manuscript A, as in chapter 4, where the Septuagint has cyrios ho theos (κύριοσ ὁ θεὸσ), meaning "lord the god," Genizah manuscript A has yyy (״׳), indicating that the name was previously in the Hebrew translation at this point. The Greek term appears to be a translation of the term adonai ha'elohim (אֲדֹנָי הָאֱלֹהִים), meaning "lord of the gods," found in the Aramaic sections of Daniel, which were generally translated as cyrion ton theon (κύριον τὸν θεὸν), meaning "Lord the god," in the

Septuagint's version. In the sections of Daniel which were translated into Hebrew, the term Yehvah elohim (יְהוָה אֱלֹהִים) is found where the Septuagint has "lord the god" (κύριον τὸν θεὸν), which confirms that the Hasmoneans substituted the name Yhůh where they found the term adonai as they were translating the texts into Hebrew.

According to the Talmud, this was to repair the damage King Manasseh had done 600 years earlier when he removed the name Yahweh from the Israelite texts, however, no evidence has survived from the era of Manasseh or earlier that proves the name was originally in the text, suggesting it was an attempt by the first Hasmonean King/High Priest Simon the Zealot to create a national Judean religion with a god having a name similar to the Roman god Jupiter (Jovis). Some other elements of the hedonistic version of Judaism remain in the Wisdom of Joshua ben Sira, including the reference to Iaw acquiring Israel as his portion when the Highest God divided the nations of humanity between the princes. This reference is found in chapter 17:

> In the division of the nations of the Earth, he set a prince over every people, and Israel is Iaw's portion, who, being his firstborn, he nourished with discipline, and giving him the light of his love does not ignore him.

This is a reference to the 70 or 72 princes who were placed over the 70 or 72 nations of humans, in the early Second Temple era hedonistic form of Judaism. This was first mentioned in the Song of Moses, in Deuteronomy chapter 32, and then again in the Talmud which mentions the story of Dobiel, the 'prince of Persia' who was once the proxy for Gabriel in heaven for 21 days after Gabriel angered God by allowing the Judeans to leave Babylon when God wanted the Babylonians to kill them. While he was Gabriel's proxy Dobiel allowed the Persians to conquer the known world, which was the explanation for the sudden rise of the Persian Empire in the early Second Temple era. Dobiel was again referred to as the "Prince of Persia" in the Revelation of Metatron, which listed Samael as the "Prince of Rome." The religion of the 70, seems to have disappeared during the Persian era, meaning the quoted proverb must date back to centuries before Joshua's time.

This is not the only book in the Septuagint to contain these curious anachronisms, the Wisdom of Solomon identified the Lord as the Sun and stated that everyone should pray to the east at dawn, something else that Josiah banned in 4th Kingdoms. While the Wisdom of Solomon can be dismissed as being anachronistic if it is older than generally assumed, this is not possible for the Wisdom of Joshua ben Sira, as he could not have lived much before 200 BC. The references to the peoples that Joshua hated, support his existence after the time of Ezra the scribe, and not much before the time of the Maccabean Revolt. He specifically mentions 3 groups, the Samaritans, the Gentiles, and the "fools at Shechem."

Not all manuscripts have this exact list, Genizah manuscript B includes the term yŭšby šôyr (יושבי שעיר), meaning "inhabitants of Seir" instead of Samaritans (Σαμαρείασ). Most scholars have accepted that "Samaritan" was a mistranslation since the Genizah manuscripts were published, as Shechem, which is mentioned at the end of the list, is in Samaria, and there is no reason to list them as two separate peoples. However, Joshua did state that the third group was not a people, which suggests the "foolish people in Shechem" was a reference to the Samaritan priesthood, which was based in Shechem.

In the early centuries of the Christian era, additional books were added to the Septuagint as appendixes, including the Book of Odes. The book is mostly a collec-tion of older songs and prayers found in the Septuagint, however, it was not made from the Septuagint's transla-tions, but from Theodotion's translation of circa 200 AD. Theodotion's translation was not from the Aramaic texts, but the Hasmonean Dynasty's Hebrew translation, resulting in some textual differences between the songs in Odes and the versions of them in the older books of the Septuagint, especially in Exodus.

The Book of Odes includes the older Prayer of Manasseh, which was found in some copies of the Septuagint, but not all. The Prayer of Manasseh is believed to have been added to one of the early versions of the Septuagint before the Maccabean Revolt, but removed before the final official version of 132 BC. The current scholarly view is that it was likely written in Greek, and is not the original Prayer of Manasseh mentioned in the Septuagint's 2ⁿᵈ Paralipomenon, however, translations of the versions found in the Septuagint are the only version found in the various translations of 2ⁿᵈ Paralipomenon, including the Syriac and Ge'ez translations, which supports the version in the Septuagint as being in the Aramaic translations the Greeks translated. Fragments of a different Prayer of Manasseh have been discovered among the Dead Sea Scrolls, written in Hebrew, which is probably a translation of a Phoenician Prayer of Manasseh. It is unclear which Prayer of Manasseh is the original, and both could be original prayers by Manasseh, who was reported as being a Judahite king from the era when the Judahites were writing in Phoenician, and taken north to Assyria where Aramaic was the common form of writing. The story of his capture is not corroborated by Assyrian sources, and seems unlikely, leaving the question of where the Aramaic prayer came from.

The 5th century Codex Alexandrinus includes the Prayer of Manasseh as one of the 14 Odes, appearing directly after Psalms, however, it often appears at different positions within Bibles and is treated as a separate work by many Christian denominations. Jerome's Vulgate, the 4th century Latin translation of the Bible, included the Prayer of Manasseh at the end of 2nd Chronicles (2nd Paralipomenon), where it also appears in the Ge'ez translation. In addition to the Greek translation, ancient copies survive in Armenian, Latin, Ge'ez, Old Slavonic, and Syriac, all of which are translations of the Septuagint's version, and not the version found among the Dead Sea Scrolls.

The Prayer of Manasseh is unusual in that it is written by one of the "evil" kings of Judah, who restored Baalism, and restored the statue of Ba'al to King Solomon's Temple. It is a prayer dedicated to the "Lord" which is a direct translation of the title "Ba'al," and may, therefore, be seen as a Baalist prayer. This is something that has concerned Jews and Christians throughout history, which is why it is not universally considered canon by either Jews or Christians.

The author of the Septuagint's 2nd Paralipomenon (Masoretic Divrei-hayyamim) attempted to resolve the question of Manasseh's prayer by adding a story of his repentance and return to worshiping the Lord after being imprisoned by the King of Assyria, however, that story is not viewed as possible by many, as it would have meant that Judah was conquered by the Assyrians, who then incarcerated the Judahite king in Nineveh. There are no records of this, however, Manasseh is mentioned as the King of Judah in the Assyrian records, and the two nations appear to have had cordial relations. The fact that the author of 2nd Paralipomenon felt he needed to explain the existence of the Prayer of Manasseh, proves it was in use by Judeans at the time, although, it may not be the Prayer that ended up in the Septuagint. Fragments of a Hebrew Prayer of Manasseh have been found among the Dead Sea Scrolls, however, not enough of them survive to determine how much the two prayers originally deviated.

Most of the other songs and prayers in the Book of Odes are copied from other books found in the Septuagint. These songs and prayers include works attributed to Moses, Hannah the mother of Samuel, King Hezekiah, the prophets Habakkuk, Isaiah, Jonah, Azariah, Hananiah, and Mishael. Additionally, the Odes include specifically Christian and Nazarene prayers from the Gospel of Luke or written by Zechariah the father of John the Baptist, Simeon, and in some manuscripts Mary the God-Bearer.

The other "original" work within the Odes is the Morning Hymn, in Chapter 14. This hymn was likely copied from something, like the rest of the book, but it is not clear where it came from. It is certainly a Christian hymn, referencing the Gospel of John 1:29:

> Behold the Lamb of God who takes away the sin of the world.

As all Christian references in the Odes are to either the Gospels of Luke or John, the two gospels originating in Anatolia, it is likely that the collection of the Odes originated there as well. This would place their origin sometime after 120 AD, in a non-Marcionite Church. Given the schisms within Christianity at the time in Anatolia, it is easy to see why the Odes were not widely adopted. Given the fact that the group of prayers included works attributed to women, it seems more likely that they were in use by the Montanists than the proto-Orthodox churches, however, this cannot be proven conclusively. Furthermore, the fact that Theodotion's translation appears to have been used indicates that Odes was compiled after 200 AD.

The earliest Greek-speaking Christians used the Septuagint exclusively, as far as the Israelite scriptures were concerned, and as a result, it is impossible to even understand the chronology of the world they described unless using the Septuagint. It is unclear why the Septuagint, Masoretic Texts, and Samaritan Asatir each contain a different chronology of the world. Adding the Book of Jubilees, and various variations of the Torah found within the Dead Sea Scrolls, there are no less than six ancient Judeo-Samaritan chronologies. The Septuagint's Cosmic Genesis includes an additional millennium of human history that was dropped from the Proto-Masoretic Texts in order to align the creation of the world with the beginning of the age of El, when the constellation Taurus became the marker of the northern vernal equinox, in 3760 BC.

The Bull El was the dominant god of the Canaanite pantheon until circa 1700 BC, when Attar the Goat (Aries) and Yam the Sea-Monster (Cetus) fought for domination of the world beneath the sky, ultimately both being replaced by the god of thunder Ba'al Hadad, in the Canaanite Ba'al Cycle. Traditional Western Christian and Jewish interpretations of the timeline within the Masoretic texts is further hampered by the so-called "missing years" of Rabbinical Time, in which hundreds of years of the Persian Empire are skipped over in order to make the timeline fit into the era since 3760 BC, a problem Christian chronologists have never had as Christianity developed after the astrology of Babylonian-era Judaism had been forgotten.

By the 4th century some Christian scholars were debating whether they should retranslate the Old Testament from the version the Jews were using, and some even suggested using the Samaritan version. Both suggestions were generally dismissed as heretical, as Jesus and the Apostles had quoted from the Septuagint, even though they had access to the Hebrew version then in use. This argument held in the West until the Middle Ages when Catholic Bibles switched to the Masoretic texts. In the east, Orthodox Bibles continued to use the Septuagint, as they do today. To the south, the Ethiopian Tewahedo Church continued to use the Septuagint, and across Asia, the Thomas Christians and Nestorians continued to use the Septuagint. Only in Western Europe were the later Masoretic texts adopted, abandoning the more ancient Septuagint, on the assumption that the Jews had copied their texts more faithfully than the Greeks had translated them. This assumption was carried forward into the Protestant Churches that broke off from the Catholic Church, and therefore almost all Protestant Bibles use the Masoretic texts for the basis of the Old Testament.

Unfortunately, this means that the earliest Christian writings are generally confusing and ignored by Protestants and Catholics. The earliest Christians of the first and second centuries quoted books that are no longer in the Bible, and as such, their writings are not always understood. Septuagint: Wisdom of Joshua ben Sira and Odes is part of a series of 21st century translations aimed at correcting this problem.

One of the problems with academic translations of the Septuagint is the use of unfamiliar names or terms, as the Septuagint was written in Greek, and therefore many names are unrecognizable to modern readers who are used to Hebrew-derived names. This project uses the more commonly understood Hebrew-derived names instead of their Greek translations, such as Canaan instead of Chanaan, and Melchizedek instead of Melchisedec. Common modern names are also used instead of either Greek or Hebrew terms when geographical locations are known, such as the archaeological name Uruk instead of the Greek Orech, or the Hebrew Erech, and the archaeological term Sumer instead of Shinar or Senar. While this could be argued as not being a correct academic procedure, it does fulfill the goal of making the translation easy to read and understand.

Wisdom of Joshua ben Sira: Prologue

While many great things have been given to us
through the law and the prophets, and by others that
have followed them, for which Israel should also be
commended for learning wisdom. Not only will the
readers need to become skillful themselves, but also those
who desire to learn must be able to benefit those who are
without through both speech and writing. My grandfather Joshua,[1] when he had studied the Orit,[2] the
prophets, and other books of our forefathers a great deal,
and had gained from them good judgment, decided to
write something himself about learning wisdom,
intending that those who want to learn, and are addicted
to learning, might gain much more by following the
Orit.

Let me ask you to read it favorably and attentively,
and to pardon us, for our shortcomings in some words,
which we have labored to translate, as the same things
stated in Aramaic[3] and translated into another language
do not have the same impact in them. Not only this, but
the Orit itself, and the prophets, and the rest of the books,
have a large difference when they are spoken in their
original language. After moving to Egypt in year 38 of
King Euergetes,[4] and living there for several years, I
found no books of minor wisdom, and therefore I
thought it most necessary for me to use some diligence
and struggle to translate it, using great carefulness and

skill to complete the book, and make it available for those, who in a foreign country, are willing to learn, and are prepared to live following the Orit.

Wisdom of Joshua ben Sira: Prologue Notes

1 Codex Sinaiticus: Iêsous (ιHϲΟΥϲ). Generally transliterated as Jesus.

Iêsous ('Ιησοῦσ) was the Greek transliteration of the Aramaic name Yšûô (ישוע). The medieval Hebrew equivalent was Yeshua' (יֵשׁוּעַ), commonly transliterated as Joshua. The name is generally translated as variants of 'Jesus' in Christian translations of this book, and is translated as Yeshua' in the Hebrew translation. As the book originated in either Aramaic or Hebrew, the appropriate English transliteration is Joshua, which is similar to both the Hebrew and Aramaic pronunciation.

2 Codex Sinaiticus: nomou (ΝΟΜΟΥ). Translation: law (or custom, ordinance)

Given that this "law" is followed by a reference to the prophets, it's clear the Torah or Orit was the "law" in question. The Orit was the common Aramaic version of the Torah during the Persian and Greek eras, which would have been the version Joshua ben Sira had access to.

3 Codex Sinaiticus: Ebraesti (εβρΑιϲΤι). Translation: Hebrew (or Aramaic)

Both Hebrew and Aramaic were referred to as Ebraesti (Εβραιστὶ) for several centuries during the Greco-Roman era. Based on the terminology within Joshua ben Sira, it appears that the original text was written in Aramaic.

4 Codex Sinaiticus: Eyergetou (ⲈⲨⲈⲢⲄⲈⲦⲞⲨ). Generally transliterated as Euergetes.

Ptolemy VIII Euergetes II Tryphon, more commonly called Ptolemy VIII Physcon today, was the King of Egypt between 169 and 164 BC, then again between 144 and 132 BC, and then again between 126 and 116 BC. His rule of Egypt was repeatedly interrupted by disputes with his older brother Ptolemy VI Philometor and his sister Cleopatra II. While his rule was interrupted repeatedly, he counted the years of his reign continuously from 170 BC, this would mean the translator moved to Egypt in 132 BC.

Wisdom of Joshua ben Sira: Chapter 1

Sophia[1] comes from Iaw[2] and is with him forever. Who can count the sand of the sea, or the drops of rain, or the days of eternity? Who can learn the height of the sky, or the width of the Earth, or the depth, and or wisdom?

Before everything, Sophia was created, and has understood prudence since eternity. The words of the Highest God[3] are the fountain of Sophia, and her ways are everlasting commandments.

The source of wisdom[4] is revealed to whom? Who knows her wonderful feats? To whom has the knowledge of Sophia been shown? Who has understood her great experience?

There is one, wise and greatly terrifying,[5] sitting on his throne. Iaw himself created her and saw her, and counted her, and poured her out on all his works. She lives in all flesh due to his gift, and he has given her to those who love him.

Revering Iaw[6] is honorable and glorious, and joy, and a crown of celebration. Revering Iaw makes a joyous heart and brings happiness, gladness, and a long life. Whoever reveres Iaw, it will go well with him in the end, and he will be blessed on the day of his death.

Revering Iaw is the beginning of wisdom, and it was created for the faithful in the womb. She builds an ever-lasting foundation within men, and she will continue with their descendants. Revering the Lord is the fullness of Sophia and fills men with her fruits. She fills their house with desirable things, and with her their property increases.

Revering Iaw is a crown of Sophia, making peace and perfect health flourish, both of which are the gifts of God. It enlarges the joy of those who love him.

Sophia rains down skill, and knowledge of understanding, and raises them to honor that hold tight with her. The root of wisdom is to revere Iaw, and her branches are long life. Revering Iaw drives away iniquities, and where it is present, it turns away anger. A furious man can't be justified, for the sway of his fury will be his destruction. A patient man will cry for a time, and afterward, joy will spring up in him. He will hide his words for a time, but the lips of many will declare his wisdom. The parables of knowledge are the treasures of Sophia, but godliness is an abomination to a sinner. If you desire wisdom, keep the commandments, and Iaw will give her to you, for revering Iaw is wisdom and instruction, and faith and meekness are delightful to him.

Don't doubt revering Iaw when you are poor, and don't come to him with a double heart. Do not be a hypocrite in the sight of men, and pay attention to what you say. Don't praise yourself, in case you fall, and bring dishonor on your mind, and Iaw discovers your secrets and throws you down among the congregation because you did not honestly revere Iaw, but your heart was full of deceit.

Wisdom of Joshua ben Sira: Chapter 1 Notes

1 Codex Sinaiticus: Sophia (ⲥⲟⲫⲓⲁ). Translation: Sophia (or wisdom, Chachamot)

The name Sophia (Σοφία) is a Greek translation, and the term is rendered as Chachamot (חָכְמוֹת) in the Masoretic literature revolving around Solomon. The author likely used its Aramaic equivalent. Chachamot is a feminine plural indefinite form of chacham (חָכָם), meaning "wise" or "smart." The Aramaic word ḥkm (חֲכַם) likewise meant "to be wise," however, the plural infinite implies the meaning "wisdom," and the feminine form implies a goddess of wisdom. While the term probably originated in a redaction of the name of Asherah from the Solomon literature, by Joshua ben Sira's time the term would have meant the "spirit of wisdom" or "principle of intelligence," and not the goddess. Both the books attributed to Solomon and the writing of Joshua ben Sira contributed greatly to the development of Gnosticism, as the angel or aeon named Sophia was derived from interpretations of their writings. As the term used here denotes a sentient being, the Greek Sophia is used in this translation.

2 Codex Sinaiticus: Cyriou (ⲔⲨⲢⲒⲞⲨ). Translation: lord (or main, chief, dominant, master)

- Genizah manuscript B: yyy (ᵐᵐ). Translation: Yhŭ

The word meaning "lord" is used inconsistently within the Wisdom of Joshua ben Sira, sometimes as a name and sometimes as a title. Modern Greek translations render it as "Lord" (Κυρίου) and "the lord" (τὸν κύριον). Given that the author and translator both lived in Judea before using the name was banned by the Hasmonean Dynasty, it is likely that the name Yhŭ (𐤉𐤅𐤄) or Yhŭh (𐤉𐤄𐤅𐤄) depending on the language of the text was originally in the book, either of which would have been translated into Greek as Iaô (Ιαω). Genizah manuscript B uses the medieval Jewish substitute for the name yyy (''') where the term "lord" is used as a name in the Septuagint, which indicates the name must have been in the original text, as not translator would both add and redact the name. The fact that Genizah manuscript B uses three yods (''') suggests that the Aramaic name Yhŭ (𐤉𐤅𐤄) was probably in the original text, and not the Judahite name Yhŭh (𐤉𐤄𐤅𐤄).

The pronunciation of the name has always been debated, which is likely why the Hasmonean King/High Priests banned the name from general use, and was a contributing factor to the Christians removing the name from their scriptures. According to Origen of Alexandria in the late 2ⁿᵈ century AD the Canaanite variant (𐤉𐤄𐤅𐤄), which he referred to as the "most ancient script," was the most accurate. According to Theodoret of Cyprus in the 5th century, Samaritans pronounced the name as Yabe (Ιαβε) or Yabai (Ιαβαι). In the 1300s BC, a Canaanite god named Yů (𓊖) was mentioned in the Ugaritic Texts, but does not appear to have been popular in northern Canaan, as little was recorded of him. As Aaron, the first cohen of Yhůh, was a priest in the Egyptian city of Iunu before the Exodus, the name almost certainly originates with the north Egyptian word for the moon, Îôh (☾), which when treated as the name of the lunar god in Iunu, was modified to Îôhů (𓇌𓃀𓈖𓂋). Like the early depictions of Yhůh in Samaria, Îôhů was depicted as being a calf, which Aaron is reported to have built a statue of shortly after the Israelites left Egypt. As the name's pronunciation and therefore spelling has been debated for over 2000 years, the earliest Latin transliteration of Iaw, derived from the Aramaic Yhů (𐡉𐡄𐡅) via the Greek Iaô (Ιαω), is used in this translation.

3 Codex Sinaiticus: theô hypsistô (ΘΕѠ ΥΨΙCΤѠ).
Translation: god highest
The Highest is a reference to God, or a god, found in many ancient religions in the region. According to the Torah, the ancient people of Salem worshiped El Elyon, which translates as "Highest God" when Abraham passed through the region. The term is also found in reference to a god worshiped by the Arameans in the Sefire I Treaty from circa 750 BC.

4 Codex Sinaiticus: sophias (ⲥⲟⲫⲓⲁⲥ). Translation: wisdom (or skill, cleverness, knowledge)

5 Codex Sinaiticus: phoberos (ⲫⲟⲃⲉⲣⲟⲥ). Translation: terrifying (or fearful, timid)

6 Codex Sinaiticus: phobos (ⲫⲟⲃⲟⲥ). Translation: awe (or reverence, fear, terror, alarm, fright, panic)

Wisdom of Joshua ben Sira: Chapter 2

Son, if you come to serve Iaw, prepare your mind for temptation. Set your heart straight, constantly endure, and don't rush away in times of trouble. Cling to him, and don't abandon him, so you may be increased at your final end. Whatever happens to you take cheerfully, and be patient when you are changed to a low estate. Gold is purified in fire, and acceptable men in the furnace of adversity. Believe in him, and he will help you and organize your path correctly. Trust in him.

You who revere Iaw, wait for his mercy and don't go astray, in case you fall. You who revere the Lord, believe him, and your reward will not fail. You who revere Iaw, hope for good and everlasting joy and mercy. Look at the generations of old, and see. Whoever trusted in Iaw and was shamed? Who persevered in the reverence of Iaw and was forgotten? Whoever called on him and was ignored?

The Lord is full of compassion and mercy, patience, very compassionate, and forgives iniquities, and saves in times of affliction. Pity the fearful hearts with timid hands, and the sinner who goes two ways! Pity him who is timid, as he does not believe, and will therefore not be defended. Pity you who have lost patience! What will you do when the Lord visits you?

They who revere Iaw will not disobey his words, and they who love him will follow his ways. They who revere Iaw will seek that which is good, pleasing to him and they who love him will be filled with the Orit. They who revere Iaw will prepare their hearts, and humiliate their minds in his sight, saying, "We will fall into the hands of Iaw, and not into the hands of men, for as his greatness is, so is his mercy."

Wisdom of Joshua ben Sira: Chapter 3

I listened to your fathers, children, and if you do this you may be safe. Iaw has given the father honor over the children and has confirmed the authority of the mother over the sons. Whoever honors his father makes atonement for his iniquities. He who honors his mother is like one who stores up treasure. Whoever honors his father, has joy from his own children, and when he prays, he will be heard. He who honors his father has a long life, and he who is obedient to Iaw will be a comfort to his mother. He who reveres Iaw will honor his father and will serve his parents like they were his owners.

Honor your father and mother both in word and deed, so a blessing may come on you from them. The blessing of the father establishes the houses of children, but the curse of the mother roots out the foundations. Don't glory in the dishonor of your father, for your father's dishonor is no glory to you. The glory of a man is from the honor of his father, and a mother in dishonor is an insult to the children.

Son, help your father in his old age and don't give him problems as long as he lives. If his understanding fails, have patience with him, and don't despise him when you are in your full strength. The knowledge of your father will not be forgotten, and instead of sin, it will be counted to build you up. On the day of your affliction, it will be remembered, and your iniquities will also melt away like ice in warm weather. He who forgets his father is like a blasphemer, and he who angers his mother is cursed by Iaw.

Son, carry on with your business in meekness, so you will be beloved by he who is approved. The greater you are, the more you should humiliate yourself, and you will find favor before Iaw.[1] Many are in high places and are famous, but mysteries are revealed to the meek. The power of the Lord is great, yet he is honored by the lowly.

Don't seek out things that are too hard for you, or search for the things that are above your strength. Think about what you are told with reverence, for you do not need to see with your eyes the things that are secret. Do not be curious about unnecessary matters, for more things are shown to you than men understand. Many are deceived by their own vain opinion, and an evil suspicion has overcome their judgment. Without eyes you will lack light, so don't profess knowledge that you don't have. A stubborn heart will be judged evil in the end, and he who loves danger will perish then. An obstinate heart will be laden with sorrows, and the wicked man will heap sin on sin. In the punishment of the proud, there is no remedy, for the plant of wickedness has taken a source in him. The heart of the prudent will understand a parable, and an attentive ear is the desire of a wise man. Water will quench a flaming fire, as alms will make an atonement for sin. He who returns good favors is mindful of that which may come after this, and when he falls, he will find peace.

Wisdom of Joshua ben Sira: Chapter 3 Notes

1 Codex Sinaiticus: cyriou (ⲕⲨⲢⲓⲞⲨ). Translation: lord (or master, owner)

• Genizah manuscript A: âlhym (**אלהים**). Translation: goddesses (in Hebrew, or gods in Aramaic, or god in Neo-Assyrian)

The word in the Genizah manuscripts is commonly translated as "God," but is a plural form of the Aramaic âlhå (𐡍𐡕𐡋𐡍), meaning "gods," or a plural form of the Hebrew elah (אֱלָה) meaning "goddesses."

The terms âlhym (𐤀𐤋𐤄𐤉𐤌) and âlhym (𐡄𐡋𐡕𐡍) are also direct transcriptions of the Neo-Assyrian word elium (𒀭𒈨𒌋), which by the Iron Age meant 'god,' indicating that text had previously been written in cuneiform, and was translated into Aramaic or Phoenician during the Iron Age.

During the Bronze Age, the word alium (𒀭𒈨𒌋) referred to a specific god, ^{deity}Ān (𒀭𒀭) the highest god, and father of the other gods. His Akkadian name was derived from the word elûm (𒂊𒈨𒌋), meaning "higher," as the term was intended to convey the meaning of "highest." He was believed to live in the polar region of the sky, where the modern constellation of Draco is located, making him the highest in the sky, around which all the gods (stars) circled.

The term El elyovn (אֵל עֶלְיוֹן), meaning 'highest god,' was translated into Hebrew in Bereshít (Masoretic Cosmis Genesis) Chapter 14, where the Greeks translated it as theô tô hypsistô (θεω τω ὑψίστω), also meaning "highest god." El Elyon is known to have been a major god of the Canaanites, called ål ůålyn (𐤀𐤋 𐤏𐤋𐤉𐤍), meaning "God and Highest" in an Aramaic language Sefire Treaty from circa 750 BC. The Greek translations of Sanchuniathon's bronze age writing that have survived to the present, referred to the primordial creator god of the Canaanites as Elioun (Ελιουν), which appears to be the same god. According to Sanchuniathon, Elioun was the highest (ὑψιστος) god, who made the sky and the land, and they made the rest of the gods.

During the Old Babylonian and Old Assyrian eras, the gods Marduk and Ashur, the national gods of Babylon and Assyria, replaced the Akkadian An as the primary god of the Mesopotamian pantheons, and by the Iron Age, the word elium had come to mean 'god,' explaining why the Aramaic term ålhym (𐤀𐤋𐤄𐤉𐤌) would have been interpreted as "god," by the Greeks.

Wisdom of Joshua ben Sira: Chapter 4

Son, don't defraud the poor from his wages, and don't make the needy wait long. Don't make a hungry one sad, or provoke a man in his distress. Don't add more trouble to a heart that is vexed, and don't hold back giving to he who is in need. Don't reject the supplication of the afflicted, or turn your face to ignore a poor man. Don't ignore the needy, and never give him the occasion to curse you, for if he curses you in the bitterness of his mind, his prayer will be heard by he who made him. Acquire the love of the congregation, and bow your head to important men. Don't let it bother you to listen to the poor, and give his meekness a friendly answer. Save him that has been treated wrongly from the hands of the proud, and do not be timid in your mind. Be merciful to the fatherless when judging, like a father, and like a husband to their mother. You will be like the obedient son of the Highest, and he has more mercy on you than a mother.

Sophia inspires life in her children, protects those who search for her and will go ahead of them in the way of justice. He who loves her loves life, and who watches for her, will embrace her sweetness. They who hold her fast will inherit life, and wherever she enters, Iaw will give a blessing.

They who serve her will be servants of Qetesh,[1] and the Lord loves those who love her. He who listens to her will judge nations, and he who sees her will remain safe. If he trusts her, he will inherit her, and his generation will be assured. She walks with him in temptation, but she tests him first. She will bring against him fear and dread and trial, and she will scourge him with the affliction of her discipline, until she tests him by her laws, and trusts his mind. Then she will strengthen him, and make a direct path to him, and give him joy, and will disclose her secrets to him, and will heap on him treasures of knowledge and understanding of justice. If he goes astray, she will forget him, and deliver him into the hands of his enemy.

Son, observe the time and run from evil. Do not be ashamed in your mind to speak the truth. For there is a shame that brings sin, and there is a shame that brings glory and grace. Accept no person against your own person, or against your mind a lie. Don't be happy when your neighbor falls, and don't refrain from speaking in the time of salvation. Don't hide your wisdom in her beauty, for by the tongue Sophia is discerned, and understanding, knowledge, and learning by the words of the wise, and steadfastness in the works of justice. In noway speak against the truth, but be ashamed of the lie of your ignorance. Do not be ashamed to confess your iniquities, but do not submit yourself to every man for sin. Don't resist against the face of the mighty, and do not strive against the stream of the river. Strive for justice for your mind, and fight for justice even to death, and Lord the god[2] will overthrow your enemies for you.

Do not be hasty in your tongue, and slack and remiss in your works. Do not be like a lion in your house, terrifying those of your household, and oppressing those who are under you. Don't let your hand be stretched out to receive, and closed when you should give.

Wisdom of Joshua ben Sira: Chapter 4 Notes

1 Codex Sinaiticus: agiô (ܐܪܝܘ). Translation: devoted (or holy, sacred, pious)

• Genizah manuscript A: ḥyym (חיים). Translation: living (or alive)

The term the Greeks translated as hagiô (ἁγίω) and hagios (ἅγιοσ), meaning "holy" or "saint," was translated into Hebrew in other books as qdůš (קדוש), a word meaning "consecration" or "sanctification," which the Masoretes later simplified to kadosh (קָדוֹשׁ), a word meaning "holy" or "sacred." The earlier Hebrew translation of qdůš (קדוש), as retained in the Aleppo Codex and Dead Sea Scrolls is also one of the Hebrew transliterations of the Canaanite title qedesh, qdš (𐤒𐤃𐤔) in the Phoenician script, and qdš (ܩܕܫ) in Aramaic. The Canaanite title was also treated as the Egyptian title of

Hathor during the Canaanite and Hyksos dynasties, qdš (𓏏𓊖𓎡). The more common transliteration of the Egyptian title is Qetesh, which, like Qedesh in Canaan, was sometimes treated as a proper name for the goddess.

The title qedesh was used in Canaan throughout the Egyptian New Kingdom era for the local goddess considered the equivalent of Hathor, the Egyptian sky-goddess. In the Ugaritic texts, from the late Bronze Age, the title was applied to the wife of El, and the mother of the gods. In the Ugaritic text, El had two wives Ôṯtrt (𒌋𒌋𒌈𒈹𒈠), later called Asherah (עֲשְׁתֹּרֶת), and Ôṯtrt ym (𒌋𒌋𒌈𒈹𒈠𒅀), later called Astarte (𐤕𐤓𐤕𐤔𐤏). These two goddesses both appear to have been fertility goddesses, Asherah being the goddess of rainwater, which was believed to fall from the stars bringing life to the land, and Astarte being the goddess that created life under the sea. In the Greek translation of Sanchuniathon's Phoenician History, reportedly written in Egypt during the New Kingdom Era, El was interpreted as the Titan Cronos, and Asherah was interpreted as the Titaness Rhea, the Titan of fertility and the night sky, who was also the mother of the gods in the early Greek religion.

In Jerusalem, Asherah was worshiped in Solomon's Temple until Josiah's reforms of circa 625 BC, along with her husband Ba'al (the sun) and their son Adon (the moon). In Baalbek, Astarte continued to be worshiped as the mother of Adon (originally the moon and later the planet Mercury) and wife of Ba'al (the sun), later called Jupiter (but still considered to be the sun) until the Roman era. Cronus and Rhea diminished in importance during the early Greek Era with the rest of the Canaanite Titans as the Greek gods supplanted them, except in Cyprus, where the local version of Astarte and Adon became the Greek gods Aphrodite (the planet Venus) and Adonis (the planet Mercury).

Joshua ben Sira is using the title qodesh in reference to Sophia, who he claims was the first thing created, something many later Gnostic sects incorporated into their beliefs. In chapter one, he also referred to Sophia's roots and branches, implying she was a tree, and suggesting that King Josiah's attempt to destroy Asherah worship had not been successful, even though he had destroyed all the Asherah trees in Judah.

2 Codex Sinaiticus: cyrios o theos (ΚΥΡΙΟϹΟΘΕΟϹ).
Translation: lord the god

• Genizah manuscript A: yyy (ייי). Translation: Yhů

This term appears to be a direct translation of the term adonai ha'elohim (אֲדֹנָי הָאֱלֹהִים), meaning "lord of the gods," found in the Aramaic sections of Daniel, which were generally translated as cyrion ton theon (κύριον τὸν θεὸν), meaning "Lord the god," in the Septuagint's version. This strongly indicates that Joshua ben Sira's original work was in Aramaic, like most of the Judean literature of the era.

Wisdom of Joshua ben Sira: Chapter 5

Set your heart on your goods, and never say, "I have enough in my life."

Don't follow your own mind and your strength, and walk in the ways of your heart. Don't say, "Who will dictate my actions to me?" as Iaw will certainly revenge your pride.

Don't say, "I have sinned, yet what harm has come to me?" as the Lord is patient, but he will in no way let you escape.

Concerning appeasement, be afraid of compounding sin to sin. Don't say, "His mercy is great, and he will be pacified for my many iniquities," as both mercy and anger come from him, and his indignation rests on sinners.

Don't be slow to turn to Iaw, and don't delay to another day, as the anger of Iaw will come suddenly, and your security will be destroyed, and perish in the day of vengeance.

Don't set your heart on goods gained unjustly, as they will not benefit you in the day of calamity.

Don't winnow with every wind, and don't go in every direction like a sinner that has a double tongue.

Be steadfast in your understanding, and let your word be the same.

Be quick to listen, and let your life be honest, and answer with patience.

If you are knowledgeable, answer your neighbor, if not, keep your mouth closed.

Both honor and shame are in speech, and the tongue of man is his downfall.

Do not be called a whisperer, and don't lie in wait with your tongue, for a foul shame is on the thief and an evil condemnation on the double tongue.

Do not be ignorant of anything whether great or small.

Wisdom of Joshua ben Sira: Chapter 6

Don't become an enemy instead of a friend, and earn a bad name in doing so along with shame and reproach. A sinner who has a double tongue will do this.

Don't praise yourself in the thoughts of your heart, that your mind does not become torn in pieces like a bull going off on its own. You will eat up your leaves, lose your fruit, and leave yourself like a dry tree.

A wicked mind will destroy him that has it and will make him be laughed at derisively by his enemies. The sweet language will multiply friends, and an honest tongue will increase kind greetings.

Be in peace with many, nevertheless have only one counselor in a thousand.

If you would take a friend, test him first and do not be quick to credit him, for some man is a friend for his own reasons, and will not stay in the days of your trouble. There is a friend, who once turned to enmity and strife will discover your reproach. Again, some friends are companions at the table, and will not continue in the day of your trouble, yet in your prosperity, he will be like you and will be bold over your servants. If you are brought low, he will be against you and will hide from your face.

Separate yourself from your enemies, and pay attention to your friends. A faithful friend is a strong defense and he who has found one has found a treasure. Nothing contravenes a faithful friend, and his honesty is invaluable. A faithful friend is the medicine of life, and those who revere Iaw will find him. Whoever honors Iaw will direct his friendship correctly, for as he is, so will his neighbor also be.

Son, gather instructions from your youth onward, so will you find Sophia in your old age. Come to her like one that plows and sows, and wait for her good fruits, for you will not struggle much in labor regarding her, but you will eat of her fruits soon. She is very unpleasant to the uneducated, and he who is without understanding will not remain with her. She will lie on him and test him like a heavy stone, and he will throw her from him before too long. Sophia is just like her name, and she is not known to many.

Listen my son, and receive my advice, and don't refuse my counsel. Put your feet into her shackles, and your neck into her chains. Bow down your shoulder, and carry her, and do not be bothered with her shackles. Come to her with your whole heart, and keep her ways with all your power. Search, and seek, and she will be made known to you, and once you have caught her, never let her go. In the end, you will find her in peace, and that will be a joy for you. Then her shackles be a strong defense for you, and her chains a robe of glory. There is a golden ornament on her, and her bands are purple lace. You will put her on like a robe of honor and will put her around you like a crown of joy.

Son, if you are willing, you will be taught, and if you will apply your mind, you will be prudent. If you love to listen, you will receive understanding, and if you apply your ear, you will be wise.

Stand in the multitude of the elders, and cling to he who is wise.

Be willing to hear every just discourse, and don't let the understanding of parables escape you. If you see a man of understanding, go to him and let your footwear out the steps of his door.

Let your mind be on the ordinances of Iaw and meditate continually in his commandments, he will establish your heart, and give you wisdom at your own desire.

Wisdom of Joshua ben Sira: Chapter 7

Do no evil, so no harm will come to you. Abandon injustices, and iniquity will turn away from you.

Son, don't sow in the fields of injustices, and you will not reap from them seven times as much.

Don't ask for authority from Iaw, nor from the king a seat of honor.

Don't justify yourself before Iaw, and before of the king have no wisdom.

Don't try to become a judge unless you can remove iniquity, or else at some point you fear a mighty person, which would be a stumbling block in the way of your justice.

Don't offend the multitude of a city, and you will not throw yourself down among the people.

Don't compound one sin with another, thinking in one you will not be unpunished.

Don't say, "He will see the many sacrifices I offer to the Highest God, and he will accept them."

Don't be timid when praying, or neglect to give alms.

Don't mock and laugh at any man in his time of trouble, as there is one who humbles and exalts.

Don't devise a lie against your brother, or your friend. Don't be willing to lie in any way, as it is not a good habit.

Don't speak much in the presence of your elders, and don't babble when you pray.

Don't hate the work or laborers or farmers, who the Highest has ordained.

Don't count yourself among the multitude of sinners, and remember that anger will not last long. Humiliate your spirit greatly, for the vengeance of the unjust is fire and worms.

Don't break your agreements with a friend, defer to any wealth, or be unfaithful to a brother even for the purest gold of Sauvira.[1]

Don't ignore a wise and good wife, for her grace is greater than gold. When your slave works honestly, don't treat him evilly, or the employee that places his life in your hands. Love a wise slave as you love your own mind, and don't defraud him of his liberty.

Do you have livestock? Keep an eye on them, and if they are a benefit to you, keep them near you.

Do you have children? Instruct them, and have them bow their heads from their youth.

Do you have daughters? Protect their body, and don't allow yourself to be attracted to them. Marry your daughter well, and you have performed a great deed, so give her to a wise man.

Do you have a wife helpful to your mind? Don't ignore her, and don't give yourself to a casual woman.

Honor your father with your whole heart, and don't forget the sorrow of your mother. Remember that you were made by them. How can you repay them for the things that they have done for you?

Revere the Lord with all your mind, and revere his priests. Love with all your strength he who made you, and don't ignore his ministers. Revere the Lord and honor his priests, and give him his portion, as it is commanded of you: the first fruits, and the trespass offering, and the gift of the shoulders, and the sacrifice of sanctification, and the first fruits of the holy things.

Stretch your hand out to the poor, so your blessing may be perfected. Alms has grace in the sight of every living man, and will not detain you among the dead.

Don't fail to consolidate those who cry, and mourn with those who mourn.

Do not be slow to visit the sick, for that will make you beloved. In all your works, remember your final destination, and you will never sin.

Wisdom of Joshua ben Sira: Chapter 7 Notes

1 Codex Sinaiticus: Souphir (ⲥⲟⲩⲫⲓⲣ)

• Genizah manuscript A: Åûpyr (אופיר)

• Genizah manuscript D: Åûpyr (אופיר)

This country's name was transliterated as Sôphêra (Σωφηρα) in 2nd Kingdoms, while Masoretic Samuel calls it Ofir (אוֹפִיר), the same spelling as found in Genizah manuscript's A and D.

The location of this civilization has been a matter of debate for centuries. Given the list of items imported from Sôphêra/Ofir, it was likely the ancient Pakistani Kingdom of Sauvira on the Indus River. Imported items include gold, silver, sandalwood, pearls, ivory, apes, and peacocks. Sandalwood trees are indigenous to South and Southeast Asia and have traditionally been considered sacred by the Hindus, Jainists, Buddhists, and Zoroastrians. Peacocks are indigenous to South and Southeast Asia, as well as the Congo rainforest, however, Sandalwood trees are not found in the Congo rainforest.

Apes were still living in South and Southeast Asia circa 1000 BC, along with most of Africa. An alternate theory regarding the location of Sôphêra was that it was a trading port in Southern Arabia or Somalia, however, the ships of Solomon were said to take three years to travel between Edom and

Sôphêra/Ofir, which makes the location of Sauvira more likely. The Kingdom of Sauvira is listed in ancient Late-Vedic texts and early Buddhist literature, as well as the Mahabharata, based around its capital of Rohri in the modern Pakistani state of Sindh. This civilization is recorded as having existed from the Early Vedic period, before 1100 BC, meaning it would have existed in the time of Solomon. In the context of this book, the gold of Sauvira likely refers to a land of gold that had become mythical since Sauvira no longer existed.

Wisdom of Joshua ben Sira: Chapter 8

Don't fight with a strong man, in case you fall into his hands.

Don't be at odds with a rich man, in case he overcomes you, for gold has destroyed many, and perverted the hearts of kings.

Don't struggle with a man who is quick with his tongue, and don't heap wood on his fire.

Don't joke around with a vulgar man, in case your ancestors are disgraced.

Don't insult a man who turns from sin, but remember that we are all worthy of punishment.

Don't dishonor a man in his old age, as we all get old.

Don't celebrate your greatest enemy's death, but remember that we all die.

Don't hate the discussions of the wise, but acquaint yourself with their proverbs, for through them you will learn instruction, and how to serve great men with ease.

Don't miss the discussions of the elders, for they also learned from their forefathers, and from them you will learn to understand and to give appropriate answers.

Don't kindle the coals of a sinner, in case you are burnt with the flame of his fire.

Don't rise in anger at the presence of a violent person, in case he lies in wait to trap you in your words.

Don't lend to him that is mightier than yourself, as if you lend to him, consider it lost.

Don't take responsibility for more than you can handle, and if you are responsible, make sure to pay it.

Don't judge against a judge because he judges according to that which is just.

Don't engage in business with a noisy man or hot-headed man, as he will do according to his own will, and you will perish with him through his foolishness.[1]

Don't struggle with an angry man, and don't go with him into a solitary place, for blood is nothing in his sight, and where there is no help, he will attack you.

Don't consult with a fool, as he can't keep counsel.

Do nothing secret in front of a stranger, as you don't know what he will do.

Don't open your heart to every man, in case he repays you shrewdly.

Wisdom of Joshua ben Sira: Chapter 8 Notes

1 This is closely paralleled in the Wisdom of Amenemope, Chapter 12: "Make no undertaking in company with the

noisy, hot-headed man, or you will be making yourself a friend of a man of moral obliquity." This is one of several verses that suggest Joshua's work was a collection of proverbs he'd copied from older works.

Wisdom of Joshua ben Sira: Chapter 9

Don't be jealous regarding your wife's body, and don't teach her an evil lesson against yourself.

Don't give your mind to a woman to walk all over you.

Don't meet with a prostitute, in case you fall into her trap.

Don't use the company of a woman who is a singer, in case you are taken with her charms.

Don't gaze at a girl, in case her beauty trips you up.

Don't give your mind to prostitutes, or you may lose your inheritance.

Don't look around yourself in the streets of the city, or wander solitary through them.

Look away from a beautiful woman, and don't look at the beauty of another, for many have been deceived by the beauty of a woman whose love is started like a fire.

Don't ever sit with another man's wife, or lay down on a bed with her, or talk with her over wine, in case your heart becomes inclined to her, and through which your desires lead you to destruction.

Don't ignore an old friend, for the new one is not comparable to him. A new friend is like new wine, but when it is old, you will drink it with pleasure.

Don't envy the glory of a sinner, for you don't know what will be his end.

Don't delight in the thing that the unjust take pleasure in, but remember they will not go unpunished to their grave.

Stay far from the man who has the power to kill, so you will not doubt the fear of death, and if you come to him, make no mistakes in case he takes away your life. Remember that you travel among traps and that you walk on the battlements of the city. As best you can, beware of your neighbor, and consult with the wise.

Talk with the wise, and be prudent in your communication in the law of the Highest.

Let just men dine with you, and let your glorying be in revering law.

Commend the hands of the artisan for his work, and the wise ruler of the people for his speech.

A man with an ill tongue is dangerous in his city, and he who is quick to talk will be hated.

Wisdom of Joshua ben Sira: Chapter 10

A wise judge will teach his people, and the governance of a prudent man is well-ordered. As the judge of the people is himself, so are his officers, and what kind of man the ruler of the city is, so are all those that live there. An unwise king destroys his people, but through the prudence of those who are the authorities the city will be inhabited. Power over the Earth is in the hand of Iaw, and in due time he will place over it one that is beneficent. In Iaw's hands is the prosperity of man, and in the body of the scribe, he will lay his honor.

Don't carry hatred for your neighbor for every wrong, and do nothing at all to injure him. Pride is hateful to Iaw and man, and by both does one commit iniquity. Because of unjust dealings, injuries, and riches are acquired through deceit, and the kingdom is transferred from one people to another. Why are Earth and Ashes proud? There is nothing more wicked than a greedy man, as he would sell his own mind, and while he lives he has no guts. All power is only for a short life. A long sickness is a problem for a physician. The physician ends a short disease, and he who is today a king will die tomorrow. Once a man is dead, he will inherit reptiles, beasts, and worms.

Pride begins when one leaves Iaw, and his heart is turned away from his creator. Pride is the beginning of sin, and he who has it will pour out abominations. Therefore Iaw brought on them strange calamities and overthrew them completely. The Lord has thrown down the thrones of proud princes and set up the meek in their place. The Lord has ripped out the roots of the proud nations and planted the lowly in their place. The Lord overthrew the countries of the heathens and destroyed them to the foundations of the earth. He took some of them away and destroyed them, and has made their memory cease from the earth.

Pride was not made for men, nor was furious anger made for those who are born of a woman. They who revere the Lord are a sure seed, and those who love him are an honorable plant. Those who don't regard the Orit, are a dishonorable seed, and they who transgress the commandments are a dishonorable seed. Among brothers, he who is chief is honored, and in his eyes, so are those who revere Iaw. Revering Iaw is the glory of the rich, and honorable among the poor. Whether he is rich, noble, or poor, their glory is revering Iaw.

Do not despise the poor man who is wise, or praise the unjust man who is rich. Great men, judges, and poten-tates will be honored, yet there are none of them greater than he who reveres the Lord. The free will serve the slave who is knowledgeable, and a man who is prudent and well instructed will not complain when he is reproved, yet he who is ignorant will not be honored.

Do not praise yourself in your business, and don't brag in the time of your distress. Better is he who labors and abounds in all things than he who brags about himself yet lacks bread.

Son, praise your mind in meekness and give it honor according to your dignity. Who will justify his iniquities against his own mind? Who will honor him who dishonors his own life? The poor man is honored for his skill, and the rich man is honored for his riches. If he is honored in poverty, how much more in riches? He that is dishonorable when rich, how much more in poverty?

Wisdom of Joshua ben Sira: Chapter 11

Sophia raises the head of he who is considered low and makes him sit among great men. Don't praise a man for his beauty, or abhor a man for his outward appearance. The bee is little among those that fly, but her fruit is the sweetest of things. Don't boast of your clothing and garments, and don't exalt yourself in the day of honor, for the works of Iaw are wonderful, and his work among men is unknown.

Many kings have sat down on the ground, and one that was never considered has worn the crown. Many mighty men have been greatly disgraced, and the honorable delivered into other men's hands. Don't lay blame before you have examined the truth. Understand first, and then rebuke. Don't answer before you have heard the case, nor interrupt men during their debate. Don't struggle in a matter that is not your concern, and don't sit in judgment with sinners.

Son, don't meddle in many matters, as if you are rich you will not be innocent. If you chase after it, you will not obtain it, and if you run from it, you will not escape it. There is an unjust man who labors, and rushes in sorrow, and is always in need. Again, there is another man who is lazy and needs help, lacking ability, and very impoverished, yet the eyes of Iaw see him, lifted him up from his low state, and lifted his head from misery. Many that saw from him in peace over all the wealth and adversity, life and death, poverty and riches, come of Iaw and were amazed.

Wisdom, knowledge, and understanding of the Orit, are from Iaw. Love, and the way of good works, are from him. Error and darkness had their beginning together with sinners, and evil will grow old with those who glory in it. Iaw's gift remains with the unjust, and his favor brings prosperity forever. There is that which grows rich by his cautiousness and stinginess, and this is the portion of his reward. When he says, "I have found peace, and now will eat continually of my goods," he does not know when the time will come on him that he must leave those things to others, and die. Be steadfast in your covenant, and be conversant in it, and grow old in your works.

Don't marvel at the works of sinners, but trust in the Lord, and live in your labor, for it is an easy thing in the sight of Iaw to suddenly make a poor man rich. The blessing of Iaw is in the reward of the just, and suddenly he makes his blessing flourish. Don't ask, "What benefit is there of my service?" and "What good things will I have from now on?"

Also don't state, "I have enough, and possess many things. What troubles will I have from now on? In the day of prosperity, there is a forgetting of affliction, and in the day of affliction, there is no more memory of prosperity. For it is an easy thing to Iaw in the day of death to reward a man according to his ways. The affliction of an hour makes a man forget pleasure, yet in his end, his actions will be discovered. Judge none blessed before his death, for a man will be known by his children.

Don't bring every man into your house, for the deceitful man has many caravans. Like a partridge taken and kept in a cage, so is the heart of the proud, and like a spy, he watches for your fall. He lies in wait and turns good into evil, and in things, worthy praise will lay blame against you. From a spark of fire, a heap of coals is ignited, and a sinful man lays in wait for blood. Pay attention to a mischievous man, for he works wickedness, in case he brings on you a perpetual blot. If you receive a stranger into your house and he will disturb you, and turn you out of your own home.

Wisdom of Joshua ben Sira: Chapter 12

When you do good, know to whom you do it so you will be thanked for your benefits. Do good to the just man, and you will find a repayment, if not from him, from the Highest. Nothing good will come to he that is always occupied by evil, or to him that gives no alms. Give to the just man, and don't help a sinner. Do well to him that is lowly, but don't give to the unjust. Hold back your bread, and don't give it to him, in case he attacks you afterwards, and you receive twice as much evil for all the good you have done for him. The Highest hates sinners, and will repay vengeance to the unjust, and keeps them against the mighty day of their punishment.

Give to the good, and don't help the sinner. A true friend can't be determined in prosperity, and an enemy can't be hidden in adversity. In the prosperity of a man, enemies will be grieved, but in his adversity, even a friend will leave. Never trust your enemy, for as iron rusts, so does his wickedness. Though he humiliates himself, and bows low, yet pay attention and beware of him, and you will be for him as if you had wiped a mirror, and you will know that his rust has not been altogether wiped away.

Don't raise him up next to you, in case, he overthrows you and takes your place. Don't let him sit at your right hand, in case he seeks to take your seat, and you, in the end, remember my words and be pricked but the thing. Who will pity a charmer that is bitten with a serpent, or anyone who has approached wild animals? One that goes to a sinner, and is defiled by his iniquities, who will pity him? He will live with you for a while, but if you begin to fall, he will not remain. An enemy speaks sweetly with his lips, but in his heart, he imagines how to throw you into a pit. He cries with his eyes, but if he finds an opportunity, he will not be satisfied with blood. If adversity comes on you, you will find him there first, and though he pretends to help you, he will undermine you. He will shake his head, and clap his hands, and whisper much, and change his attitude.

Wisdom of Joshua ben Sira: Chapter 13

He who touches pitch will be defiled by it, and he who associates with a proud man will become like him.

Don't burden yourself more than you need to while you live, and don't associate with one who is mightier and richer than yourself, as, how will the kettle and the earthen pot agree together? If the one is struck against the other, it will be broken.

If a rich man has done wrong, he can still threaten everyone. If the poor is wronged, he must still beg. If you are beneficial to him, he will use you, but if you have nothing, he will ignore you. If you have anything, he will live with you, and he will make you broke, and will not be sorry for it. If he needs you, he will lie to you and smile at you, and put you in hope. He will speak to you nicely, and ask, "What do you want?"

He will reduce you through his foods until he has drawn you dry two or three times, and in the end, he will laugh at you insultingly, and afterward, when he sees you, he will ignore you, and shake his head at you.

Beware that you do not be deceived and brought down in your celebration. If you are invited by a mighty man, withdraw yourself, and he invites you again. Don't ask him for anything, in case you are refused. Don't stand far away, in case you are forgotten. Don't pretend to be equal to him in discussions, and don't believe his many words, for with much communication will he tempt you, and smiling at you will get your secrets. Cruelly he will remember your words, and will not spare you pain, and to put you in prison. Observe, and pay attention, for you walk in peril of your downfall.

When you hear these things, awake from your sleep. Love the Lord all your life, and call on him for your salvation.

Every beast loves his kind, and every man loves his neighbor. All flesh consorts according to kind, and a man will cling to his kind. What friendship has the wolf with the lamb? Likewise will the unjust have with the just. What agreement is there between the hyena and a dog? What peace between the rich and the poor? As the wild donkey is the lion's prey in the wilderness, so the rich will eat the poor. As the proud hate humility, so does the rich hate the poor. A rich man beginning to fall is held up by his friends, but a poor man being down is pushed away by his friends. When a rich man has fallen, he has many helpers, and he saw things not to be spoken, and yet men justify him. The poor man slipped, and yet they rebuked him too, even if he spoke wisely, yet could have no place.

When a rich man speaks, every man is quiet, and, look, what he says, they praise it to the clouds, but if the poor man speaks, they say, "Who is this guy?" and if he stumbles, they will help to overthrow him.

Riches are good for him who has no sin, and poverty is evil in the mouth of the unjust. The heart of a man changes his attitude, whether it is for good or evil, and a happy heart makes a cheerful attitude. A cheerful attitude is a token of a heart that is prosperous, and the learning of parables is a tiring labor of the mind.

Wisdom of Joshua ben Sira: Chapter 14

Blessed is the man who has not slipped with his mouth, and is not pricked with the multitude of iniquities. Blessed is he whose conscience has not condemned him, and who has not fallen from his hope. Riches do not come to the stingy, and what would an envious man do with money? He that gathers by defrauding his own mind, gathers for others who will spend his wealth without restrain. He who is evil to himself, who will he be good too? He will take no pleasure in his goods.

There is no one worse than he who envies himself, and this is a repayment of his wickedness. If he does good, he does it unwillingly, and in the end, he will admit his wickedness. The envious man has a wicked eye, and he turns away his face and despises men. A covetous man's eye is not satisfied with his portion, and the iniquity of the wicked dries up his mind. A wicked eye envies his bread, and he is stingy at his table.

Son, according to your ability be good to yourself, and give Iaw his due sacrifice. Remember that death will not be long in coming, and that the covenant of the grave is not shown to you. Do good to your friend before you die, and according to your ability stretch out your hand and give to him. Don't defraud yourself of the good days, and don't let the enjoyment of good desire pass you by. Will you not leave your troubles to another, and your labors to be divided by lot? Give, and take, and sanctify your mind, for there is no seeking of delicacies in the grave.

All flesh grows old like a garment, for the covenant from the beginning is, "You will die the death."

As of the green leaves on a thick tree, some fall, and some grow, likewise are the generations of flesh and blood, one comes to an end, and another is born. Every work rots and rusts away, and the worker of inequity will do likewise. Blessed is the man who meditated on the good things of Sophia, and that reasons justly through his understanding. He who considers her ways in his heart, will also have an understanding of her secrets. Go after her as one that hunts, and lies in wait for her ways. He who pries in at her windows will also listen at her doors. He who lodges near her house will also fasten a pin in her walls. He will pitch his tent near her and will lodge in a house where good things are. He will set his children under her shelter and will lodge under her branches. By her he will be covered from heat, and in her glory will he live.

Wisdom of Joshua ben Sira: Chapter 15

He who reveres Iaw will do good, and he who knows the Orit will obtain her.

Like a mother will she meet him, and receive him as a wife married as a virgin. With the bread of understanding will she feed him, and give him the water of Sophia to drink. He will be calmed in her, and will not be moved, and will rely on her, and will not be confused. She will exalt him above his neighbors, and among the congregation will she open his mouth. He will find joy and a crown of gladness, and she will cause him to inherit an eternal name.

But foolish men will not attain to her, and sinners will not see her. For she is far from pride, and men who are liars can't remember her. Praise is not suitable in the mouth of a sinner, for it was not sent to him from Iaw.

Praise will be spoken by Sophia, and the Lord will benefit it. Don't say, "It is because of the Lord that I fell away," for you should not do the things that he hates.

Don't say, "He has caused me to sin," for he has no needs of the sinful man.

The Lord hates all abominations, and they who revere him don't love it. He himself made man from the beginning and left him in the hand of his counsel. If you will keep the commandments, and perform acceptable faithfulness. He has set fire and water before you, stretch out your hand wherever you want. Before man is life and death, and whichever he likes will be given him.

The wisdom of the Lord is great, and he is mighty in power and sees all things. His eyes are on those who fear him, and he knows every work of man. He has commanded no man to do wickedly, neither has he given any man permission to sin.

Wisdom of Joshua ben Sira: Chapter 16

Don't desire a multitude of unprofitable children or delight in unjust sons. Though they multiply, don't celebrate them unless they revere law.

Don't trust in their lives or respect their multitudes, as one that is just is better than a thousand, and it is better to die without children than to have those that are unjust.

Through Sophia, the city will be replenished, but families of the wicked will quickly become desolate. Many things like this I have seen with my eyes and my ears have heard greater things than these. In the congregation of the unjust will a fire be started, and in a rebellious nation, anger is ignited. He was not peaceful towards the ancient giants who fell in the strength of their foolishness. Neither did he spare the place where Lot stayed, but hated them because of their pride. He did not pity the people who were carried away in their sin, nor the 600,000 infantry, who were gathered together in the hardness of their hearts.

If there is one stubborn among the people, it is a marvel if he escapes unpunished, for both mercy and anger, are with him, and he is strong enough to both forgive and to pour out displeasure. As his mercy is great, and so are his punishments. He judges a man according to his works, and the sinner will not escape with his plunder, and the patience of the just will not be frustrated. Make way for every work of mercy, for every man will receive according to his works. Iaw hardened Pharaoh, that he should not know him, and instead, his powerful works might be known to the world. His mercy is manifest to every creature, and he has separated his light from the darkness adamantly.

Don't say, "I will hide from Iaw! Will any above remember me? I will not be remembered among so many people, for what is my mind among such an infinite number of creatures?"

Look at the sky, and the sky of Shamayim,[1] the abyss, and the earth will shake when he visits. The mountains also, and foundations of the earth be shaken with trembling when he looks on them. No heart can worthily understand these things, and who is able to comprehend his ways? It is a storm that no man can see, as the majority of his works are hidden. Who can declare the works of his justice? Who can endure them? His covenant is far away, and the trial of all things comes at the end. He who lacks understanding will think about vain things, and a foolish man erring imagines follies.

Son, listen to me and learn knowledge, and mark my words with your heart. I will show the doctrine in weight, and declare his knowledge exactly. The works of Iaw are done in judgment from the beginning, and from the time he made them, he disposed of parts of them. He garnished his works forever, and in his hand are the greatest of them to all generations. They neither labor nor are weary or cease from their works. None of them hinders another, and they will never disobey his word. After this Iaw looked at the Earth and filled it with his blessings. He has covered the face of it with all manner of living things, and they will return to it again.

Wisdom of Joshua ben Sira: Chapter 16 Notes

1 Codex Sinaiticus: o ouranos cae o ouranos tou ouranou (**O OYPANOC KAI O OYPANOC TOY OYPANOY**). Translation: the sky (or Uranus) and the sky (or Uranus) of skies

• Genizah manuscript A: hšmym ûšmy hšmym (**שמי ושמים השמים**). Translation: the skies (or Shamayim) and the sky of the skies (or Shamayim)

The term ouranou (ουρανου) was used in the Septuagint as a translation for the word meaning "skies," which was translated as Shamayim (שָׁמֶיִם) in the Masoretic texts, which was also preserved in Genizah manuscript A. Shamayim was a Canaanite god of the skies.

Wisdom of Joshua ben Sira: Chapter 17

Iaw created man from the dirt and returns him to it again. He gave them a few days, a short time to have power also over the things on it. He endowed them with free will, made them in his own image, put the fear of man into all flesh, and gave him dominion over animals and birds.

He created from him a helper like himself and gave them counsel, a tongue, eyes, ears, and a heart to think with, and filled them with knowledge and under-standing. He created in them the science of the spirit, he filled their heart with Sophia and showed them both good and evil. He set his eye on their hearts to show them the greatness of his works so that they might praise the name which he has sanctified, and glory in his wondrous acts, and so that they might declare the glorious things of his works.

Besides this, he gave them the knowledge and the law of life for an inheritance. He made an everlasting covenant with them and showed them his judgments. Their eyes saw the majesty of his glory, and their ears heard his glorious voice. He said to them, "Beware of all iniquity,"

He gave every man commandments concerning his neighbor. Their ways are always before him, they are not hidden from his eyes. In the division of the nations of the Earth, he set a prince over every people, and Israel is Iaw's portion,[1] who, being his firstborn, he nourished with discipline, and giving him the light of his love does not ignore him. Therefore all their works are like the sun before him, and his eyes are continually on their way. None of their unjust actions are hidden from him, but all their iniquities are before Iaw. Iaw being gracious and knowing his work, neither left them nor forgot them, but spared them.

The alms of a man is like a signet with him, and he will remember the good actions of man as the apple of his eye. Afterward, he will rise up and reward them, and render their reward, to everyone on their heads. But to the repentant, he has given the way of justice, and he has strengthened those that were fainting in patience and has given to them the truth.

Turn to Iaw, and forget your sins. Make your prayer before the face of Iaw, and offend less.

Turn to the Highest, and turn away from your injustice, for he will lead you out of darkness into the light of health, and hate your abominations vehemently.

Who will praise the Highest in Sheol,[2] as do those who live and give thanks? Praise perishes from the dead, as from one that is not, and the living and sound in heart will praise the Lord.

How great is the mercy of the Lord, and his compassion to those that turn to him! All things can't be in men, because the son of man is not immortal. What is brighter than the Sun? Yet it is eclipsed. Flesh and blood will imagine evil, yet he views the power of the heights from the sky, and all men are but dirt and ashes.

Wisdom of Joshua ben Sira: Chapter 17 Notes

1 The reference to Iaw gaining Israel as his portion when the Highest God divided the nations of the Earth between the princes, is a legacy of the Second Temple Samaritan religion which taught that Iaw was one of the 70 or 72 princes who ruled over the 70 or 72 nations of humanity. This belief system was reflected in the Song of Moses in Deuteronomy chapter 32, and the story in the Talmud of Dobiel, the prince of Persia who was once the proxy for Gabriel for 21 days allowing the Persians to conquer the known world. The Revelation of Metatron, from the late Classical Era also includes a reference to Dobiel and Samael, the angelic princes of Persia and Rome, which proves the belief in the 70/72 princes continued throughout the Classical era, however, do not appear to have been relegated to the outskirts of Jewish philosophy.

The belief in the 70/72 princes is likely rooted in the early astrology of the Neo-Assyrian and Neo-Babylonian Eras, as most of the names of the princes that survive appear to be constellations. Dobiel, which translates as 'bear god' or 'bear of

God' was the prince of the Persians, because the Persians came from the north, and the constellation Ursa Major, the great bear, is in the northern region of the sky.

2 Codex Sinaiticus: adou (ⲀⲆⲞⲨ). Translation: Hades (or the underworld)

The Greek translation of Hades was used where the Masoretic texts retain the term She'ovl (שְׁאוֹל), the name of the underworld in ancient Israelite beliefs ruled by Mot (מָוֶת), the personification of death.

Wisdom of Joshua ben Sira: Chapter 18

He who lives forever created all things together. Iaw alone will be justified, and he remains an invincible king forever.

Who is able to describe his works? Who will search out his glorious acts? Who will show the power of his majesty? Who will be able to describe his mercy? Nothing may be removed or added, nor is it possible to learn the glorious works of the Lord.

When a man has finished, then will he begin. When he quits, he will be at a loss. What is man, and what is his grace? What is his good, or what is his evil? The number of the days of men is at the most a hundred years, they are like a drop of water of the sea, like a grain of the sand, so are a few years compared to eternity. Therefore Iaw is patient with them and pours out his mercy on them. He has seen the presumption of their heart that it is wicked, and has known their end that it is evil. Therefore has he filled up his mercy in their favor, and has shown them the way of justice.

The compassion of man is toward his neighbor, but the mercy of the Lord is on all flesh. He has mercy, teaches, and corrects like a shepherd does his flock. He has mercy on him that receives the discipline of mercy, and that makes a hurry in his judgments.

Son, in your good actions, make no complaint, and when you give anything, add no grief with an evil word. Will not the dew assuage the heat? Also, a good word is better than a gift. Is it not a word better than a gift? Both are with a justified man, but a fool will complain bitterly, and a gift of one ill-taught consumes the eyes. Before judgment, examine yourself, and learn before you speak. Before sickness, take medicine, and before judgment, examine yourself, and you will find forgiveness. Humiliate yourself before you are sick, and in the time of iniquities show repentance.

Let nothing stop you from fulfilling your vows, and do not be afraid to be justified even to death. Before making a vow, prepare your mind, and do not be a man that tempts the Lord.

Remember the anger that will be on the final day and the time of repaying when he will turn away his face. Remember poverty in the time of abundance and the needs of poverty in the day of riches. From the morning until the evening, the time will be changed, and all these are swift in the eyes of Iaw.

A wise man will fear in all he does, and in the days of sins will beware of sloth. Every man of understanding knows Sophia and will give praise to him who finds her. They that were of good understanding in words, have also done wisely themselves, and have understood truth and justice, and have poured out proverbs and judgments. Don't chase your lusts, but turn away from your own appetites. If you give to your mind her desires, she will make you a joy to your enemies. Take no pleasure in cheerful celebrations, and don't be tied to the expense of them. Make not yourself poor by borrowing to contribute to feasts when you have nothing in your purse, for you will be an enemy to your own life.

Wisdom of Joshua ben Sira: Chapter 19

A working man who is given to drunkenness will not be rich, and he who condemns small things will fall by little and little. Wine and women will make men of understanding fall away, and he who clings to prostitutes will become a fool. Moths and worms will inherit him, and a bold man will be taken away. He who is quick to give credit is light-hearted and will be lessened, and he who sins against his own mind will be despised. Whoever takes pleasure in wickedness will be condemned, but he who resists, pleasures crowns his life. He who can rule his tongue will live without problems, and he who hates gossip has less evil. Don't repeat to another that which is told to you, and you will not fare worse.

Whether it is to friend or enemy, don't talk of other men's lives, and if you can reveal them without offense, don't, as he hears and sees you, and when the time comes he will hate you. If you have heard a word, let it die with you, and be bold, and it will not burst you. A fool struggles with words, like a woman in labor with a child. Like an arrow that sticks in a man's thigh, so is a word within a fool's belly. Admonish a friend, in case he may not understand, saying, "I didn't do it," or if he did it, that he may not do it again.

Admonish your friend, as it could be he has not said it, and if he has said it, that he may not say it again.

Admonish a friend, for many times it is a slander, and don't believe every story. There is one who slips in his speech, but not in his heart, and who is he who has not offended with his tongue?

Admonish your neighbor before you threaten him, and don't be angry, and remember the Orit of the Highest. Revering Iaw is the first step to being accepted by him, and wisdom obtains his love. The knowledge of the commandments of Iaw is the doctrine of life, and those who do things that please him will receive the fruit of the tree of immortality. Revering Iaw is all wisdom, and in all wisdom is the performance of the law and the knowledge of his omnipotence.

If a slave says to his master, "I will not do as you want," even if afterward he does it, he angers the one who feeds him. The knowledge of wickedness is not Sophia nor at any time the counsel of sinners prudence. There is a wickedness and the same an abomination, and there is a fool lacking in wisdom. He that has little understanding yet reveres is better than one who has much wisdom yet transgresses the Orit of the Highest. There is an exquisite subtlety, and the same is unjust, and there is one that turns aside to make judgment appear, and there is a wise man that justifies in judgment. There is one who submits himself exceedingly with great lowliness, and there is one that casts down his countenance and pretends as if he did not see that which is unknown. Where he is not known, he will do evil before you are aware. If, for lack of power, he is stopped from injustice, when he finds an opportunity he will do evil. A man may be known by his look and one that has an understanding by his countenance when you meet him. A man's attire, excessive laughter, and gait, show what he is.

Wisdom of Joshua ben Sira: Chapter 20

How much better is it to reprove, than to be angry, and not to hinder him that confesses in prayer. The lust of a eunuch[1] will defile a young girl, and so is he who executes judgment with violence.

There is one that keeps silent and is found wise, and another by much gossiping becomes hateful. Some man holds his tongue because he has no answer, and some keep silent waiting for his time. A wise man will hold his tongue until he sees an opportunity, but a gossiper and a fool will not consider the time. He who uses many words will be hated, and he who takes for himself authority will be hated.

There is success in unjust things to a man without discipline, and there is a finding that turns to loss. There is a gift that is not profitable, and there is a gift whose repayment is double. There is an abasement because of glory, and there is one that will lift up his head from a low estate. There is he who buys much for a small price and returns the same seven-fold.

A man wise in words will make himself beloved, but the graces of fools will be poured out. The gift of the fool will do you no good, for his eyes are seven times. He will give a few things, and complain much, and when he opens his mouth kindles a fire. Today a man lends, and tomorrow he asks it back, such a man as this is hated.

A fool has no friend, and there will be no thanks for his good deeds. Those that eat his bread, are of a false tongue. How often and how many will laugh and insult him! He does not distribute with right understanding that which was to be had, in like manner also that which was not to be had. The slipping of a false tongue is as one that falls on the pavement, so the fall of the wicked will come speedily.

A man without grace is like a vain story, it will be continually in the mouth of the unwise. A parable coming out of a fool's mouth will be rejected, for he does not speak it at the right time. There is he who is hindered from sinning through poverty, yet in his peace, he will be punished. There is he who will destroy his own mind through bashfulness, and through the occasion of an unwise person will destroy it, and by the respect of people, he will destroy himself. There is that bashful promise to his friend that makes him his enemy for nothing.

A lie is a foul blot in a man, and yet it will be continually in the mouth of men without discipline. A thief is better than a man who is always lying, but both of them will inherit destruction. The manners of lying men are without honor, and their confusion is with them without ceasing. A wise man will advance himself with his words, and a prudent man will please the great ones.

He that tills his land will make a tall heap of grain, and he who works justice will be exalted, and he who pleases great men will escape iniquity. Presents and gifts blind the eyes of judges and make them dumb in the mouth so that they cannot decide correctly. The hidden wisdom or the treasure that is not seen, what profit is there in either of them? Better is he who hides his foolishness, than the man that hides his wisdom.

Wisdom of Joshua ben Sira: Chapter 20 Notes

1 Codex Sinaiticus: eunouchou (ЄΥΝΟΥΧΟΥ). Translation: eunuch

The term Joshua ben Sira probably used the Aramaic sry (𐡎𐡓𐡉), a title used during the Persian Era as a translation for the Persian term xwāja (خواجه), which translates as lord, master, owner, dignitary, wealthy man, vizier, or eunuch, as the Persians employed many eunuchs as court officials. The Aramaic translation was derived from the ancient Egyptian sr (𓋴𓂋𓀙), meaning "official" or "magistrate," via the Demotic Egyptian as srỉ ([illegible]) with the same meaning. In both Classical Hebrew saris (סָרִיס) and Coptic siour (ⲥⲓⲟⲩⲣ) meant "eunuch," also influenced by the Persian term xwāja during the Persian rule of Judea and Egypt. This indicates that the translator was more familiar with Judeo-Aramaic and Egyptian than Imperial-Aramaic and Persian.

Wisdom of Joshua ben Sira: Chapter 21

My child, if you have been unjust, don't do it again, and for your past injustices pray to be forgiven. Flee from injustice like a serpent that will bite you if you go near it, its teeth like lion's teeth destroying human lives.

All lawlessness is like a two-edged sword, and when it cuts, there is no healing. Panic and pride wipe out wealth, and so too the house of the proud is uprooted. Prayer from the lips of the poor is heard at once, and justice is quickly granted to them. Whoever hates correction walks the sinner's path, but whoever reveres Iaw repents in his heart. Quick talkers are famous, but when they slip the wise see it.

Those who build their houses with someone else's money are like those who collect stones for their funeral mounds. A band of criminals is like a bundle of wood, they will end in a flaming fire. The path of sinners is smooth flagstones, but its end is the pit of Sheol. Those who follow the Orit control their thoughts and fulfill the reverence of Iaw's wisdom.

One who is not clever can never be taught, but there is a cleverness filled with bitterness. The knowledge of the wise wells up like a flood, and their counsel like a living spring. A fool's mind is like a broken jar, it cannot hold any knowledge at all. When the intelligent hear a wise saying, they praise it and add to it. The unrestrained hear it with distaste and throw it behind their back.

A fool's gossip is like a load on a journey, but delight is to be found on the lips of the intelligent. The views of the prudent are asked for in an assembly, and their words are taken to heart. Like a house in ruins is wisdom to a fool, to the stupid, knowledge is incomprehensible noise. To the senseless, education is like shackles on the feet, like manacles on the right hand. Fools raise their voice in laughter, but the prudent at most smile quietly.

Like a gold ornament is an education to the wise, like a bracelet on the right arm. A fool steps boldly into a house, while the well-bred are slow to make an entrance. An oaf peeps through the doorway of a house, but the educated stay outside. It is rude for one to listen at a door, the discreet person would be overwhelmed by the disgrace. The lips of the arrogant talk of what is not their concern, but the discreet will carefully weigh their words.

The mind of fools is in their mouths, but the mouth of the wise is in their mind. When the godless curse their adversary, they really curse themselves. Slanderers defile themselves and are hated by their neighbors.

Wisdom of Joshua ben Sira: Chapter 22

The slothful man is like a filthy stone, everyone hisses at his disgrace. The slothful man is like a lump of dung, whoever touches it shakes it off the hands.

An undisciplined child is a disgrace to its father if it is a daughter, she brings him to poverty. A thoughtful daughter obtains a husband of her own, a shameless one is her father's grief.

She who is sexually permissive dishonors both her father and her husband, and they both will despise her.

Like music at the time of mourning is poorly-timed talk, but lashes and discipline are at all times wisdom. Teaching a fool is like gluing a broken pot or rousing another from a deep sleep. Whoever talks with a fool talks to someone asleep, and when it is over, he asks, "What was that?"

Cry over the dead, for their light has gone out, cry over the fool, for sense has left him. Cry but less bitterly over the dead, for they are at rest, worse than death is the life of a fool. Mourning for the dead, seven days, but for the wicked fool, a whole lifetime.

Do not talk much with the stupid, or visit the unintelligent. Beware of those in case you have trouble, and will be spattered when they shake themselves off. Avoid them and you will find peace and not be tired by their lack of sense. What is heavier than lead? What is its name but 'Fool'? Sand, salt, and an iron weight are easier to carry than a stupid person.

A wooden beam firmly bonded into a building is not loosened by an earthquake, likewise, the mind that is firmly resolved after careful deliberation will not be afraid at any time. The mind solidly backed by intelligent thought is like a stucco decoration on a smooth wall. Small stones lying on an open height will not remain when the wind blows, so a timid mind based on foolish plans cannot stand up to a fear of any kind.

Whoever jabs the eye brings tears, and whoever pierces the heart bares its feelings. Whoever throws a stone at birds drives them away, and whoever insults a friend breaks up the friendship. If you draw a sword against a friend, do not despair as it can be undone. Should you open your mouth against a friend, do not worry, for you can be reconciled. But a contemptuous insult, a confidence broken, or a treacherous attack will drive any friend away.

Win your neighbor's trust while he is poor, so that you may rejoice with him in his prosperity. In times of trouble, remain honest with him, so that you may share in his inheritance when it comes. The billowing smoke of a furnace precedes the fire, so insults precede bloodshed. I am not ashamed to shelter a friend, and I will not hide from him. But if harm should come to me because of him, all who hear of it will beware of him. Who will stand a guard over my mouth, an effective seal on my lips, that I may not fail through them, and my tongue may not destroy me?

Wisdom of Joshua ben Sira: Chapter 23

Iaw, father and master[1] of my life, do not abandon me to their designs, do not let me fall because of them! Who will apply the lash to my thoughts, and to my mind the cane of discipline, that my failings may not be spared or the injustices of my heart overlooked? Otherwise, my failings may increase, and my injustices may be multiplied! I fall before my adversaries, and my enemy rejoices over me?

Iaw, father and god of my life do not give me haughty eyes! Remove the evil desire from my heart. Let neither gluttony nor lust overcome me, do not give me up to shameless desires.

Listen, children, to instruction concerning the mouth, for whoever keeps it will not be trapped. Through the lips, the sinner is caught, by them the reviler and the arrogant are tripped up. Do not accustom your mouth to oaths, or habitually speak the name of Qetesh. Just as a servant constantly under scrutiny will not be without bruises, so one who swears continually by the name of Qetesh will never remain free from sin. Those who swear many oaths heap up offenses, and the scourge will never be far from their houses. If they swear in error, guilt is incurred, and if they neglect their obligation, the sin is twice as much. If they swear without reason they cannot be declared innocent, for their households will be filled with calamities.

There are words comparable to death, may they never be heard in the inheritance of Jacob. To the devout all such words are foreign, they do not wallow in sin. Do not accustom your mouth to coarse talk, for it involves sinful speech. Keep your father and mother in mind when you sit among the mighty, in case you forget yourself in their presence and disgrace your upbringing. Then you will wish you had never been born and will curse the day of your birth. Those accustomed to using abusive language will never acquire discipline as long as they live.

Two types of people multiply injustices, and a third brings down anger, burning passion is like a blazing fire, not to be quenched till it burns itself out. One unchaste with his family never stops until a fire breaks out. To the unchaste all bread is sweet, he is never through till he dies.

The man who dishonors his marriage bed says to himself, "Who can see me? Darkness surrounds me, walls hide me, and no one sees me. Who can stop me from sinning?"

He is not mindful of the Highest, fearing only human eyes. He does not realize that the eyes of Iaw, ten thousand times brighter than the sun, observe every step taken, and peer into hidden corners. The one who knows all things before they exist still knows them all after they are made. Such a man will be denounced in the streets of the city, and where he least suspects it, he will be apprehended.

So it is with the woman unfaithful to her husband, who offers him an heir by another man. First of all, she has disobeyed the law of the Highest, second, she has wronged her husband, and third, through her wanton adultery, she has brought out children by another man. Such a woman will be dragged before the assembly, and her punishment will extend to her children. Her children will not take root, and her branches will not bear fruit. She will leave behind a cursed memory, her disgrace will never be blotted out. Therefore all who live on the earth will know, and all who remain in the world will understand, that nothing is better than revering Iaw, nothing sweeter than obeying the commandments of Iaw.

Wisdom of Joshua ben Sira: Chapter 23 Notes

1 Codex Sinaiticus: despota (ⲆⲉⲤⲦⲦⲟⲦⲁ). Translation: despot (or lord, owner, master)

Wisdom of Joshua ben Sira: Chapter 24

Sophia sings her own praises, and among her people, she proclaims her glory. In the assembly of the Highest, she opens her mouth, and in the presence of his army, she tells of her glory, "From the mouth of the Highest I came out and covered the earth like a mist. In the highest sky, I lived, and my throne was in a pillar of cloud. In the vault of the sky I circled alone and walked through the deep abyss. Over waves of the sea, over all the land, over every people and nation, I held influence. Among all these, I wanted a resting place, but in whose inheritance should I live? Then the Creator of all gave me his command, and my creator chose the place for my tabernacle. He said, 'Live among Jacob, in Israel your inheritance.'"

"Before all ages, from the beginning, he created me, and through all ages, I will not cease to be. In the tabernacle, I ministered before him, and so I was established in Zion. In the city he loves as he loves me, he gave me rest, and in Jerusalem, my domain. I struck source among the glorious people, in the portion of Iaw, his inheritance."

"Like a cedar in Lebanon, I grew tall, and like a cypress on Mount Hermon. I grew tall like a palm tree in Ein Gedi. Like rosebushes in Jericho, like a fair olive tree in the field, and like a plane tree beside water I grew tall. Like cinnamon and fragrant cane, like precious myrrh I gave out perfume. Like galbanum and onycha and mastic, and like the odor of incense in the tabernacle.

"I spread out my branches like a terebinth, my branches so glorious and so graceful. I bud out delights like a vine, and my blossoms are glorious and rich fruit. Come to me, all who desire me, and be filled with my fruits. You will remember me as sweeter than honey, and better to have than the honeycomb. Those who eat of me will hunger still, those who drink of me will thirst for more. Whoever obeys me will not be put to shame, and those who serve me will never go astray."

All this is in the book of the covenant of the Highest God, the Orit which Moses commanded us as a heritage for the community of Jacob. It overflows like the Pishon[1] with wisdom, and like the Tigris at the time of first fruits. It floods over like the Euphrates with understanding, and like the Jordan at harvest time. It floods like the Nile with instruction and like the Gihon[2] in ancient times.

The first human being never finished understanding Sophia, nor will the last succeed in fathoming her. Deeper than the sea are her thoughts, and her counsels, than the great abyss. Now I, like a stream from a river, and like water channeling into a garden, I said, "I will water my plants, and I will drench my flower beds. Then suddenly this stream of mine became a river, and this river of mine became a sea. Again, I will make my teachings shine like the dawn, and I will spread their brightness far away. Again, I will pour out instruction like prophecy and give it to generations yet to come."

Wisdom of Joshua ben Sira: Chapter 24 Notes

1 Codex Sinaiticus: Phisôn (ϕⲓⲥⲱⲛ)

The name was recorded as Pishon (פִּישׁוֹן) in Bereshít, the Masoretic version of Cosmic Genesis, although the location of the river is debated. There has been speculation regarding the location of this river for over 2000 years. In the 1st century AD, the Jewish historian Flavius Josephus identified it as the Ganges in India, in his Antiquities of the Jews. The 4th century Cave of Treasures identified it as being the Indus River in Pakistan. In the 11th century AD, the Rabbi Shlomo Yitzchaki (Rashi) identified it as the Nile. It has also variously been identified as the Roini in Georgia, the Aras in the Armenian highlands, and the Amu Darya in Central Asia. Most of these locations have been suggested based on older commentaries from Jewish and Israelite communities spread across the old Persian Empire. Rashi's theory ultimately derived from Egyptian-Israelite commentary regarding the name Pachnamunis (Παχναμουνίς), a major city in the Sebennytos district of the Nile Delta, through which one of the major tributaries of the Nile flowed in ancient times. The city was also the capital of Egypt during the 30th Dynasty

(380 to 343 BC). The name Pachnamunis seems to have originated in the Libyan 23rd Dynasty of Egypt, between 837 and 728 BC. It is composed of the words Pachn and amun (oⵏol), meaning "Pachn River" in Libyan languages.

The dominant theory today is that it was a reference to the dried river bed of a major river that once flowed across the Arabian Peninsula from the mountains near Medina to the old Iraqi wetlands, where the Euphrates, Tigris, and Kuran Rivers merge. Part of this river still flows seasonally today as the Wadi al-Batin (وادي البـاطن) in northeast Saudi Arabia, Kuwait, and Iraq. The Wadi al-Batin is the final section of the much longer Wadi al-Rummah dry river valley that runs across the peninsula, but is today disconnected from the Wadi al-Batin by sand dunes that have covered a section of the former river valley. When the river still flowed, it was an estimated 1,200 km (750 mi) long, and connected a number of now-dried lakes in the interior of the Arabian peninsula. It is unclear when the river last flowed its full length, but some estimates place it at 8000 BC. The wadi that runs out of the mountains near Medina still floods approximately three times a century. In 1838, the wadi overflowed and created a 520 km^2 (200 mile^2) lake that lasted for 2 years. If this name originated in Sumerian, like several other terms in Cosmic Genesis and Bereshít, then the name was probably not a name, but a description of the dried out river bed. In Sumerian, the term pronounced as pí sún (𒉿𒌋𒁲), would mean "it is destroyed." This supports the identification of the Pishon as being the dried out riverbed of the al-Rummah when the oldest form of the text was written, with the flowing river being a distant memory from an age before the great flood. Joshua's reference to the river's overflowing suggests it flooded again during his time, or that he thought it was the Nile, like Rabbi Shlomo Yitzchaki did 1200 years later.

2 Codex Sinaiticus: Gêôn (ⲅ ⲏ ⲱ ⲛ)

This river's location is debated, as the Greek identification of it flowing through Aethiopia suggests it is the Nile. In modern Sudan (Classical Aethiopia) and Ethiopia (ancient Punt) it has generally been interpreted as the Blue Nile (Abay), which was known as G^{w}azzam ('ⲧⲟ ⲏ ⳟ) in the earliest records from the region. The dominant view outside of Northeast Africa is that it was the Karun River, which flows through Khuzestan province in southwestern Iran. Identifying the Gihon as the Karun is based on the identification of Kush in the Masoretic texts as Khuzi instead of the Kingdom of Kush.

If the name Gêôn / Gîhôn is derived from the Sumerian name, the original name was probably ^{id}G̃eana (𒀀𒈾𒈾𒀀), meaning "^{river}flowing in rocks," similar to the Sumerian name for the Tigris: ^{id}Idigna (𒀀𒄘𒁇), meaning "^{river}flowing rough," and the Sumerian name for the Euphrates: ^{id}Buranun (𒀀𒌓𒄒𒉣), meaning "^{river}Copper source." The Euphrates was the source of copper for the Sumerian civilization, and the Tigris is a rough fast-flowing river, while the Karun flowed down through the Zagros Mountains into the plains of Khuzistan before flowing into the old Sumerian wetlands in southern Iraq.

As Joshua ben Sira refers to the Gihon as having flooded in ancient times, yet, neither the Karun nor the Blue Nile had stopped flowing, it suggests that Joshua ben Sira thought the Geon was another river, such as the Black Nile, the modern Atbarah-Tekezé River, which had already become seasonal by the era of Joshua, or the Red Nile, the modern Mareb River, which had already dried to the point of being a seasonal wadi. The Atbarah-Tekezé River flows into the Nile north of the Blue Nile, as a steam in the dry season, and a river in the wet season, and is the northernmost surviving tributary of the Nile. The Mareb River no longer reaches the Nile, except in years with unusually high rainfall, when it floods down the dried-out riverbed, and merges with the Atbarah shortly before the Atbarah reaches the Nile. In dynastic Egyptian records, both rivers could be navigated by barge, as could the Yellow Nile that flowed into the Nile to the west from Darfur.

Wisdom of Joshua ben Sira: Chapter 25

[Sophia continued,] "In three things I was beautified, and stood up beautiful both before Iaw and men: the unity of brothers, the love of neighbors, and a man and a wife that agree together."

"I hate three kinds of men, and I am greatly offended by their life: a poor man who is proud, a rich man who is a liar, and an old adulterer who is uncritically fond."

"If you have gathered nothing in your youth, how can you find anything in your age? How beautiful is judgment in gray hairs, and for ancient men to know counsel! How beautiful is the wisdom of old men, and understanding and counsel to men of honor? Experience is the crown of old men, and revering Iaw is their glory."

"There are nine things which I have judged in my heart to be happy, and the tenth I will describe with my tongue: A man that has joy in his children, he who lives to see the fall of his enemy, he who lives with a wise wife, he who has not slipped with his tongue, he who has not served a man more unworthy than himself. He who has found prudence, he who speaks in the ears of those that will listen, he who finds Sophia, and yet, is there none above him that reveres the Lord. Reverence of Iaw passes all things for illumination and he who remembers it, what will he be compared to? Revering the Lord is the beginning of his love, and faith is the beginning of clinging to him."

"Give me any plague except the plague of the heart and any wickedness except the wickedness of a woman. Any affliction except the affliction from those that hate me, and any revenge except the revenge of my enemies. There is no head above the head of the serpent, and there is no anger above the anger of an enemy. I would rather live with a lion and a dragon than live in a house with a wicked woman."

"The wickedness of a woman changes her face and darkens her attitude like sackcloth. Her husband will sit among his neighbors, and when he hears it will sigh bitterly. All wickedness is small compared to the wickedness of a woman. Let the portion of a sinner fall on her. Like climbing up a sandy path is to the feet of the aged, so is a wife full of words to a quiet man. Stumble not at the beauty of a woman, and desire her not for pleasure."

"A woman, if she supports her husband is full of anger, impudence, and a great deal of shame. A wicked woman abates the courage and makes a heavy attitude and a wounded heart. A woman who will not comfort her husband in distress makes weak hands and feeble knees. From woman came the original sin, and because of her, we all die. Give the water no passage, nor a wicked woman her liberty to seek pleasure. If she does not do as you would have her, cut her off from your flesh, and divorce her, and let her go."

Wisdom of Joshua ben Sira: Chapter 26

[Sophia continued,] "Happy is the husband of a good wife, and the number of his days will be doubled. A loyal wife brings joy to her husband, and he will finish his years in peace. A good wife is a generous gift bestowed on him who reveres Iaw. Whether rich or poor, his heart is content, and a smile is always on his face."

"There are three things I dread, and a fourth which terrifies me:

Public slander, the gathering of a mob, and false accusations are all harder to carry than death.

A wife jealous of another wife is heartache and mourning, everyone feels the lash of her tongue.

A wicked wife is a chafing yoke, taking hold of her is like grabbing a scorpion.

A drunken wife arouses great anger as she does not hide her shame."

"An unchaste wife can be recognized by her haughty stare and her painted eyelids. Keep strict watch over a headstrong daughter, lest, when she finds liberty, she uses it to her hurt. Watch out for her impudent eye, and do not be surprised if she betrays you. As a thirsty traveler opens his mouth and drinks from any water nearby, so she sits down before every tent peg and opens her quiver for every arrow."

"A gracious wife delights her husband, her thought-fulness puts flesh on his bones. A silent wife is a gift from Iaw, and nothing is worth more than her self-discipline. A modest wife is a supreme blessing, and no scales can weigh the worth of her chastity. Shemesh will rise as the highest lord.[1] The beauty of a good wife is in her well-ordered home. The light which shines above the menorah is a beautiful face on a stately figure. Golden columns on silver bases, at her shapely legs and steady feet."

"My child, keep intact the love of your youth and do not give your strength to strangers. Seek out a fertile field from all the land, and sow it with your own seed, confident in your fine stock, and your offspring will prosper, and grow great, confident in their good descent."

"A woman for hire is seen as valuable as saliva, but a married woman is a deadly trap for her lovers. An unjust wife will be given to the lawless man as his portion, but a just wife will be given to the man who reveres Iaw. A shameless woman wears out reproach, but a virtuous daughter will be modest even with her husband. A headstrong wife is thought of as a bitch, but the one with a sense of shame reveres Iaw. The wife who honors her husband will seem wise to everyone, but if she dishonors him in her pride, she will be known to everyone as unjust. Happy is the husband of a good wife, for the number of his years will be doubled. A loud-mouthed and chatty wife will be regarded as a trumpet sounding the charge, and every person who lives like this will spend his life in the anarchy of war."

"Two things bring grief to my heart, and a third arouses my anger: The wealthy are reduced to poverty, the intelligent are held in contempt, and those who pass from righteousness to sin. The Lord prepares the sword for them."

"A merchant can hardly keep from wrongdoing, nor can a shopkeeper stay free from sin."

Wisdom of Joshua ben Sira: Chapter 26 Notes

1 Codex Sinaiticus: Hêlios anatellôn en hypsistoes Cyriou (ΗΛΙΟC ΑΝΑΤΕΛΛѠΝ ΕΝ ΥϯΙCΤΟΙC ΚΥΡΙΟΥ). Translation: Helios (or sun) will rise (or rise up, cause to grow, give birth to, bring to light) in (or at, on, during) highest lord

• Genizah manuscript C: šmš - bmrůmy môl (שמש - במרומי מעל). Translation: Shemesh (or sun) – in the heights above.

Helios was the translation used in the Septuagint for the Canaanite god of the sun, Shemesh, preserved as Shamesh

(שֶׁמֶשׁ) in the Leningrad Codex, and Šmš (שמש) in Genizah manuscript C.

Wisdom of Joshua ben Sira: Chapter 27

[Sophia continued,] "Many have sinned for a small matter, and he who seeks abundance will turn his eyes away. Like a nail holds fast between the joints of the stones, likewise, sin sticks close between buying and selling. Unless a man holds himself diligently in revering Iaw, his house will soon be overthrown. Like when a sieve is shaken, the husks appear, so do people's faults when they speak. The furnace tests the potter's vessels, but the test of a person is in conversation. The fruit of a tree shows the care it has had, and so speech shows the bent of a person's heart."

"Praise no one before he speaks, for it is then that people are tested. If you struggle for justice, you will attain it and wear it like a splendid robe. Birds nest with their own kind, and honesty comes to those who work at it. A lion lies in wait for prey, like sin waits for evil-doers. The conversations of the just are always wisdom, but the fool changes like the moon. Limit the time you spend among the stupid, but frequent the company of the wise. The conversation of fools is offensive, and their laughter like immoral sins."

"Their oath-filled talk makes the hair stand on end, and their disputes make one plug their ears. The wrangling of the proud ends in bloodshed and their cursing is painful to hear. Whoever betrays a secret destroys confidence, and will never find a congenial friend. Love your friend, and stay faithful to him, and if you betray his secrets, do not go after him. For as one might kill another, you have killed your neighbor's friendship. Like a bird released from your hand, you have let your friend go and cannot recapture him. Don't chase after him, for he has left and has escaped like a gazelle from a trap. A wound can be bandaged, and an insult can be forgiven, but whoever betrays secrets does hopeless damage. Whoever has shifty eyes plots mischief and those who know him will keep their distance. In your presence, he uses honeyed talk and admires your words, but later he changes his tone and twists the words to ruin you. I have hated many things, but not as much as him, and the Lord hates him as well. A stone falls back on the head of the one who throws it high, and a treacherous blow causes many wounds."

"Whoever digs a pit falls into it, and whoever lays a trap is caught in it. The evil anyone does will recoil on him without knowing how it came on him. Mockery and abuse will befall the arrogant, and vengeance lies in wait for them like a lion. Those who rejoice in the downfall of the just will be caught in a trap, and pain will consume them before they die. Anger and rage, these also are abominations, yet a sinner holds on to them."

Wisdom of Joshua ben Sira: Chapter 28

The vengeful will face Iaw's vengeance, and indeed he remembers their injustices in detail. Forgive your neighbor the wrong done to you when you pray, your own injustices will be forgiven. Does anyone nourish anger against another and expect healing from Iaw? Can one refuse mercy to a sinner like oneself, yet seek pardon for one's own injustices?

If a mere mortal cherishes anger, who will forgive his injustices? Remember your final days, set enmity aside, and remember death and decay, and cease from sin! Remember the commandments and do not be angry with your neighbor, and remember the covenant of the Highest, and overlook faults. Avoid strife and your injustices will be fewer, for the hot-tempered kindle strife.

The sinner disrupts friendships and sows discord among those who are at peace. The more the wood, the greater the fire, the more the cruelty, the fiercer the strife, the greater the strength, the sterner the anger, the greater the wealth, the greater the anger.

Pitch and resin make fire flare up, and a hasty quarrel provokes bloodshed. If you blow on a spark, it turns into a flame, if you spit on it, it dies out, yet you do both with your mouth!

Cursed are gossips and the double-tongued, for they destroy the peace of many.

A gossiping tongue subverts many and makes them refugees among people. It destroys strong cities and overthrows the houses of the great. A gossiping tongue drives virtuous women from their homes and robs them of the fruit of their struggle. Whoever listens to it will find no rest, nor will they live in peace.

A blow from a whip raises a welt, but a blow from the tongue will break bones. Many have fallen by the edge of the sword, but not as many as by the tongue. Happy the one who is sheltered from it, and has not endured its anger, who has not borne its yoke or been bound with its chains. Its yoke is a yoke of iron, and its chains are chains of bronze. The death it inflicts is an evil death, even Sheol is preferable to it.

It has no power over the just, or they will be burned in its flame, but those who forsake Iaw will fall victim to it, as it burns among them eternally. It will hurl itself against them like a lion, and like a leopard, it will tear them to pieces. As you fence in your property with thorns, so make a door and a bolt for your mouth.

As you lock up your silver and gold, also make balances and scales for your words. Take care not to slip by your tongue and fall victim to one lying in ambush.

Wisdom of Joshua ben Sira: Chapter 29

The merciful lend to their neighbor, by holding out a helping hand, they keep the commandments. Lend to your neighbor in his time of need, and pay back your neighbor on time. Keep your promise and be honest with him, and at all times you will find what you need.

Many borrowers ask for a loan which causes trouble for those who help them. Until he gets a loan, he kisses the lender's hand and speaks softly of his creditor's money, but at the time of payment, delays, makes excuses, and finds fault with the timing. If he can pay, the lender will recover barely half and will consider that a windfall. If he cannot pay, the lender is cheated of his money and acquires an enemy at no extra charge. With curses and insults, the borrower will repay, and instead of honor will repay with abuse.

Many refuse to lend, not out of meanness, but from fear of being cheated needlessly, but with those in humiliated circumstances be patient, do not keep them waiting for your alms. Because of the commandment, help the poor, and in their need, do not send them away empty-handed. Lose your money for a relative or friend, do not hide it under a stone to rot.

Dispose of your treasure according to the commandments of the Highest, and that will profit you more than the gold. Store up alms in your treasury, and it will save you from every evil. Better than a mighty shield and a sturdy spear it will fight for you against the enemy.

A good person will be responsible for a neighbor, but whoever has lost a sense of shame will fail him. Do not forget the kindness of your backer, for he has given his very life for you. A sinner will turn the favor of a pledge into misfortune, and the ungrateful will abandon his rescuer. Being irresponsible has ruined many who were prosperous and tossed them about like waves of the sea.

It has exiled the prominent and sent them wandering through foreign lands. The sinner will come to grief through responsibility, and whoever undertakes too much will fall into lawsuits. Help your neighbor according to your means, but take care in case you fall yourself. Life's prime needs are water, bread, and clothing, and also a house for decent privacy.

Better is the life of the poor under the shadow of their own roof than sumptuous banquets among strangers. Whether little or much, be content with what you have, then you will hear no reproach as a parasite. It is a miserable life to go from house to house, for where you are a guest you dare not open your mouth. You will entertain and provide drink without being thanked, and besides, you will hear these bitter words: "Come here, you parasite, set the table, let me eat the food you have there! Go away, you parasite, for one more worthy, and for my relative's visit I need the room!"

Painful things to a sensitive person are to be rebuked like a parasite and insults from creditors.

Wisdom of Joshua ben Sira: Chapter 30

Whoever loves a son will chastise him often, that he may be his joy when he grows up. Whoever disciplines a son will benefit from him, and boast of him among acquaintances. Whoever educates a son will make his enemy jealous, and rejoice in him among his friends. At the father's death, he will seem not dead, for he leaves after him one like himself, who he watched through life with joy, and in death, without regret.

Against his enemies, he has left an avenger, and one to repay his friends with kindness. Whoever spoils a son has wounds to bandage, and will allow heartache at every cry. An untamed horse turns out stubborn, and a son left to himself grows up unruly. Pamper a child and he will be a terror for you, indulge him, and he will bring you grief. Do not laugh with him in case you share sorrow with him, and in the end, you will gnash your teeth.

Do not give him his own way in his youth, and do not ignore his follies. Bow down his head in his youth, and beat his sides while he is still young. In case he becomes stubborn and disobeys you, and leaves you disconsolate. Discipline your son and make his yoke heavy, in case you are offended by his shamelessness. Better the poor in vigorous health than the rich with bodily ills.

I would rather have a healthy body than any gold and a content spirit than pearls. No riches are greater than a healthy body, and no happiness than a joyful heart. Better is death than a wretched life, everlasting sleep than constant illness. Good things set before one who cannot eat are like food offerings placed before a tomb.

What good is an offering to an idol that can neither eat nor smell? So it is with the one being punished by Iaw, who groans at what his eyes see. Do not give in to sadness, or torment yourself deliberately. A joyous heart is the very life of a person, and cheerfulness prolongs his days. Distract yourself and renew your courage, drive resentment far away from you, for grief has killed many, and nothing is to be gained from resentment. Envy and anger shorten one's days, and anxiety brings on premature old age. Those who are cheerful and merry at the table benefit from their food.

Wisdom of Joshua ben Sira: Chapter 31

Wakefulness over wealth wastes away the flesh, and anxiety over it drives away sleep. Wakeful anxiety banishes slumber, and it disturbs sleep more than a serious illness. The rich labor to pile up wealth, and if they rest, it is to enjoy pleasure. The poor labor for a meager living, and if they ever rest, they become needy. The lover of gold will not be free from sin, and whoever pursues money will be led astray by it. Many have come to ruin for the sake of gold, yet destruction lays before their very eyes. It is a stumbling block for fools, any simpleton will be trapped by it. Happy is the rich person found without fault, who does not turn aside after wealth. Who is he, that we may praise him?

For he has done wonders among his people. Who has been tested by gold and been found perfect? Let it be for him his glory. Who could have been unjust but did not, and could have done evil but did not? So his good fortune is secure, and the assembly will recount his praises. Are you seated at the table of the great? Bring to it no greedy gut, nor say, "How much food there is here!"

Remember that the greedy eye is evil. What has been created more greedy than the eye? Therefore, it weeps for any cause. Recognize that your neighbor feels as you do, and keep in mind everything you dislike. Regarding what he looks at, do not put out a hand, or reach for the same dish when he does.

Eat, like anyone else, what is set before you, but do not eat greedily, in case you are despised. Be the first to stop, as befits good manners, and do not gorge yourself, in case you give offense. If there are many with you at the table, do not be the first to stretch out your hand. Is not a little enough for a well-bred person? When he lies down, he does not wheeze. Moderate eating ensures sound slumber and a clear mind on rising the next day. The trouble of sleeplessness and of nausea and colic are with the glutton!

Should you have eaten too much, get up to vomit and you will have relief. Listen to me, my child, and do not mock me, later you will find my advice good. In whatever you do, be moderate, and no sickness will befall you. People bless one who is generous with food, and this testimony to his goodness is lasting. The city complains about one who is stingy with food, and this testimony to his stinginess is lasting. Don't let wine be the proof of your strength, for wine has been the ruin of many.

As the furnace tests the work of the smith, so does wine the hearts of the insolent. Wine is the very life of anyone if taken in moderation. Does anyone live who lacks wine which from the beginning was created for joy? The joy of heart, good cheer, and delight is wine enough, drunk at the proper time.

Headache, bitterness, and disgrace is wine drunk amid anger and strife. Wine in excess is a trap for the fool, and it lessens strength and multiplies wounds. Do not wrangle with your neighbor when the wine is served, or despise him while he is having a good time, say no harsh words to him or trouble him by making demands.

Wisdom of Joshua ben Sira: Chapter 32

If you are chosen to preside at a dinner, do not be puffed up, but with the guests be like one of them. Take care of them first and then sit down, see to their needs, and then take your place, and share in their joy and receive a wreath for a job well done.

You who are older, it is your right to speak, but temper your knowledge and do not interrupt the singing. Where there is entertainment, do not pour out discourse, and do not display your wisdom at the wrong time. Like a seal of carnelian in a setting of gold, a concert of music at a banquet of wine.

A seal of emerald in a work of gold, the melody of music with delicious wine. Speak, young man, only when necessary, when they have asked you more than once. Be brief, say much in a few words, and be knowledgeable and yet quiet. When among elders do not be forward, and with officials do not be too insistent.

The lightning that flashes before a hailstorm is like the esteem that shines on modesty. Leave in good time and do not be the last, go home quickly without delay. Enjoy doing as you wish, but do not sin through words of pride. Above all, bless your Creator, who showers his favors on you. Whoever seeks him must accept discipline, and whoever resorts to him obtains an answer.

Whoever seeks the law will master it, but the hypocrite will be trapped by it. Whoever reveres Iaw[1] will understand what is right, and out of obscurity, he will draw forth a course of action. The lawless turn aside warnings and distort the law to suit their purpose. The sensible will not neglect direction, the proud and insolent are deterred by no fear.

Do nothing without deliberation, then once you have acted, have no regrets. Do not go on a way set with snares, and do not stumble on the same thing twice. Do not trust the road, because of bandits, and be careful on your roads. Whatever you do, be on your guard, for whoever does so keeps the commandments. Whoever follows the law protects himself, and whoever trusts in Iaw will not be put to shame.

Wisdom of Joshua ben Sira: Chapter 32 Notes

1 Codex Sinaiticus: cyrion (ΚΥΡΙΟΝ). Translation: lord (or master, ruler, owner)

• Genizah manuscript B: yyy (ייי). Translation: Yhů

• Genizah manuscript F: -1 (ל-). This is accepted as being half of the word ål (אל), meaning 'god,' indicating that name Yhů (יהו) was substituted with both yyy (""") and "god" (אל) when it was translated into Hebrew.

Wisdom of Joshua ben Sira: Chapter 33

No evil can harm the one who reveres Iaw, through trials, again, and again, he is rescued. Whoever hates the Orit is without wisdom, and is tossed about like a boat in a storm. A prudent person trusts in the Orit, and the law for them is faithful with clear answers to questions. Prepare your words and then you will be listened to, draw on your training, and give your answer.

Like the wheel of a cart is the mind of a fool, and his thoughts are like a turning axle. A mocking friend is like a stallion that neighs, no matter who the rider may be.

Why is one day more important than another, when the same sun lights up every day of the year? By Iaw's knowledge, they are kept distinct, and he designates the seasons and feasts. Some he exalts and sanctifies, and others he lists as ordinary days. Likewise, all people are of clay, and from dirt, humankind was formed. In the fullness of his knowledge, Iaw distinguished them, and he designated their different ways. Some he blessed and exalted, and some he sanctified and drew to himself. Others he cursed and brought low, and expelled them from their place.

Like clay in the hands of a potter, to be molded according to his pleasure, so are people in the hands of their Creator, to be dealt with as he decides. As evil contrasts with good and death with life, so are sinners in contrast with the just. Consider all the works of the Highest, they come in pairs, one the opposite of the other. Now I am the last to keep vigil, like a gleaner following the grape-pickers.

Since by Iaw's blessing, I have made progress until like a grape-picker I have filled my wine press, consider that not for myself only have I labored, but for all who seek instruction.

Listen to me, leaders of the people, rulers of the congregation, pay heed! Let neither son nor wife, neither brother nor friend, have power over you as long as you live. Do not give your wealth to another, in case you must plead for support yourself. While the breath of life is still in you, let no one take your place.

Far better that your children plead with you than that you should look for a handout from them. Keep control over all your affairs, bring no stain on your honor. When your few days reach their limit, at the time of death distribute your inheritance. Fodder and whip and loads for a donkey, food, correction, and work for a slave. Make a slave work, and he will look for rest, let his hands be idle and he will seek to be free.

The yoke and harness will bow the neck, and for a wicked slave, punishment in the stocks. Force him to work so he does not become idle, for idleness teaches much mischief. Put him to work, as is fitting for him, and if he does not obey, load him with chains. But never lord it over any human being, and do nothing unjust.

If you have but one slave, treat him like yourself, for you have acquired him with your life's blood. If you have but one slave, deal with him as a brother, for you need him as you need your life. If you mistreat him and he runs away, in what direction will you look for him?

Wisdom of Joshua ben Sira: Chapter 34

Empty and false are the hopes of the senseless, and dreams give wings to fools. Like one grabbing at shadows or chasing the wind, so anyone who believes in dreams. What is seen in dreams is a reflection, the likeness of a face looking at itself. How can the unclean produce what is clean? How can the false produce what is true? Divination, omens, and dreams are unreal, and what you already expect, the mind fantasizes. Unless they are especially sent by the Highest, do not fix your heart on them, as dreams have led many astray, and those who put their hope in them have perished.

Without such deceptions, the Orit will be fulfilled, and in the mouth of the faithful is complete wisdom. A much-traveled person knows many things, and one with much experience speaks sense. An inexperienced person knows little, whereas with travel one adds to resourcefulness. I have seen much in my travels and learned more than I could ever say.

Often I was in danger of death, but by these experiences, I was saved, living like the spirit of those who revere Iaw, for their hope is in their savior. The life who reveres the Lord is afraid of nothing and is never discouraged, for he is their hope.

Happy the mind that reveres the Lord! Who does he trust, and who supports him? The eyes of Iaw are on those who love him, and he is their mighty shield and strong support. A shelter from the heat, a shade from the noonday sun, a guard against stumbling, a help against falling.

He lifts up spirits, brings a sparkle to the eyes, and gives health and life and blessing. Ill-gotten goods offered in sacrifice are tainted. Presents from the lawless are not acceptable. The Highest is not pleased with the gifts of the unjust, nor for their many sacrifices does he forgive their injustices.

One who slays a son in his father's presence, or whoever offers sacrifice from the holdings of the poor.

The bread of charity is life itself for the needy, whoever withholds it is a murderer. To take away a neighbor's living is to commit murder, and to deny a laborer his wages is to shed blood. If one builds up, and another tears down, what do they gain but trouble?

If one begs, and another curses, whose voice will the master hear? If one touches a corpse again after bathing, what does he gain by the purification? So one who fasts for injustices, but goes and commits them again. Who will hear his prayer, what is gained by mortification?

Wisdom of Joshua ben Sira: Chapter 35

To follow the Orit is to make many offerings, and whoever observes the commandments sacrifices a peace offering. By works of charity, one offers fine flour, and one who gives alms presents a sacrifice of praise.

To refrain from evil pleases Iaw, and to avoid injustice is atonement. Do not appear before Iaw empty-handed, for all that you offer is in fulfillment of the precepts. The offering of the just enriches the altar, a sweet odor before the Highest.

The sacrifice of the just is accepted, and never to be forgotten. With a generous spirit pay homage to Iaw, and do not spare your freewill gifts. With each contribution show a cheerful countenance and pay your tithes in a spirit of joy. Give to the Highest as he has given to you, generously, according to your means.

For Iaw always repays and will give back to you seven-fold but offers no bribes, and these he does not accept! Do not trust in the sacrifice of the fruits of extortion, for he is a god of justice, who shows no partiality. He shows no partiality to the weak but hears the grievance of the oppressed. He does not forsake the cry of the orphan, or the widow when she pours out her complaint. Do not the tears that stream down her cheek cry out against the one that causes them to fall?

Cultivators[1] of goodwill are accepted, and their petition reaches the clouds. The prayer of the lowly pierces the clouds, and it does not rest till it reaches its goal, nor will it withdraw till the Highest responds, judges justly, and affirms the right.

The Lord will not delay, but like a warrior, he will not be still until he breaks the backs of the merciless and wreaks vengeance on the nations, until he destroys the scepter of the proud, and cuts off the staff of the wicked, until he requites everyone according to their deeds, and repays them according to their thoughts, until he defends the cause of his people, and makes them glad by his salvation. Welcome is his mercy in times of trouble like rain clouds in times of drought.

Wisdom of Joshua ben Sira: Chapter 35 Notes

1 Codex Sinaiticus: therapeuôn (ΘЄΡΑΠΕΥωΝ). Translation: attendants (or servants, flatterers, consultants, healers, cultivators)

Wisdom of Joshua ben Sira: Chapter 36

Come to our aid, Master the god[1] of everything, and put all the dread of you in nations! Raise your hand against the foreign people, that they may see your mighty deeds. As you have shown them your sanctity through us, now use them to show us your greatness. Then they will know, as we know, that there is no god other than you, Iaw. Give new signs and work new wonders, and show forth the splendor of your hand and right arm.

Rouse your anger, pour out anger and humiliate the enemy, scatter the foe. Hurry the ending, appoint the time, and let people proclaim your mighty deeds. Let the raging fire consume the fugitive, and your people's oppressors meet destruction. Crush the heads of the hostile rulers who say, "There is no one besides me."

Gather all the tribes of Jacob, that they may inherit the land as in days of old. Show mercy to the people called by your name: Israel, which you named your firstborn. Take pity on your holy city: Jerusalem, your living place. Fill Zion with your majesty, your temple with your glory.

Give evidence of your ancient actions, and fulfill the prophecies spoken in your name. Reward those who have hoped in you, and let your prophets be proved true. Hear, Iaw, to the prayer of your servants, according to the blessing of Aaron for your people, and all who are on the earth will know that you are the Lord, the god of ages.[2] The throat can swallow any food, yet some foods are more agreeable than others. The palate tests delicacies put forward as gifts, and so does a keen mind test deceitful tidbits. One with a tortuous heart brings about grief, but an experienced person can turn the tables on him.

A woman will accept any man as a husband, but one woman will be preferable to another. A woman's beauty makes her husband's face light up, as it surpasses all else that delights the eye. If besides, her speech is soothing, her husband's lot is beyond that of mortal men.

A wife is her husband's richest treasure, a helper for himself, and a staunch supporter. A vineyard with no hedge will be overrun, and a man with no wife becomes a homeless wanderer. Who will trust an armed band that shifts from city to city? A man who has no nest, who lodges wherever night overtakes him?

Wisdom of Joshua ben Sira: Chapter 36 Notes

1 Codex Sinaiticus: despota o theos (ΔΕϹΠΟΤΑΟΘΕΟϹ). Translation: despot (or master, ruler, owner) the god

• Genizah manuscript B: ålhy (אלחי). Translation: god. The reference to the despota (δέσποτα) was dropped from the Hebrew translation.

This term appears to be a translation of the term mara ha'elohim (מְרָא הָאֱלֹהִים), meaning "master of the gods," an alternative to the term adonai ha'elohim (אֲדֹנָי הָאֱלֹהִים), meaning "lord of the gods." Mara was an alternative to adonai commonly used in Aramaic texts, however, not in Hebrew texts, supporting Joshua's writings have been in Aramaic, and not Judahite.

2 Codex Sinaiticus: cyrios i ho theos tôn aeônôn (ΚΥΡΙΟCΕΙΟ ΘΕΟC ΤωΝ ΑΙωΝωΝ). Translation: lord my the god the aeons (or centuries, ages)

• Genizah manuscript B: ål ôůlm (אל עולם). Translation: God of the world (or eternity)

The Greek term appears to be a direct translation of the Biblical Aramaic adonai ha'elah alemayya (אֲדֹנָי הָאֱלָה עָלְמַיָא), meaning "lord the god forever." The Hebrew translation in Genizah manuscript B has dropped the reference to the Lord, which was common in late Classical era Jewish translations, as the Lord was considered a Christian term at the time. This itself confirms that the Aramaic text the translation was made from could not have included the name Yhůh at this point, as the name would have been substituted with yyy (ייי).

Wisdom of Joshua ben Sira: Chapter 37

Every friend declares friendship, but some friends are friends in name only. Is it not a sorrow to death when your other self becomes your enemy?

"Alas, my companion! Why were you created to fill the earth with deceit?"

A harmful friend will look to your table, but in times of trouble, he stands apart. A good friend will fight with you against the foe, and against your enemies, he will hold up your shield. Do not forget your comrade during the battle, and do not neglect him when you distribute your spoils. Every counselor points out a way, but some counsel ways of their own.

Watch out when one offers advice, and find out first of all what he wants. For he also may be thinking of himself, and why should the opportunity fall to him? He may tell you how good your way will be, and then stand by to see you impoverished. Seek no advice from your father-in-law, and keep your intentions hidden from one who is envious of you.

Seek no advice from a woman about her rival, from a coward about war, from a merchant about business, from a buyer about value, from a miser about generosity, from a cruel person about well-being, from a worthless worker about his work, from a seasonal laborer about the harvest, from an idle slave about a great task, and pay no attention to any advice they give.

Instead, associate with a religious person, who you know keeps the commandments, and who is like-minded with yourself and will grieve for you if you fall. Then, too, heed your own heart's counsel, for there is nothing you can depend on more. The heart can reveal your situation better than seven sentinels on a tower.

Then with all this, pray to Iaw to make your steps firm in the true path. A word is the source of every deed, a thought, of every act. The source of all conduct is the heart and the four branches it shoots out. Good and evil, death and life, and their absolute mistress is the tongue. One may be wise and benefit many, yet appear foolish to himself. One may be wise, but if his words are rejected, he will be deprived of all enjoyment.

When one is wise to his own advantage, the fruits of knowledge are seen in his own person. When one is wise to the advantage of people, the fruits of knowledge are lasting. One wise for himself has full enjoyment and all who see him praise him. The days of one's life are counted, but the life of Israel, days without number. One wise among the people wins a heritage of glory, and his name lives on and on.

Son, while you are well, govern your appetite, and see that you do not allow it that which is bad for you, for not everything is good for everyone, nor is everything suited to every taste. Do not go to excess with any enjoyment, nor become a glutton for choice foods, for sickness comes with over eating, and gluttony brings on nausea. Through a lack of self-control, many have died, but the abstemious one prolongs life.

Wisdom of Joshua ben Sira: Chapter 38

Make friends with the physician as he is essential to you, and Iaw created him. Healing comes from the Highest,[1] and he will receive payment from the king. Knowledge makes the physician distinguished and gives access to those in authority. Iaw makes the earth yield healing plants which the prudent should not neglect. Was not the water sweetened by a twig so that all might learn his power?

He endows people with knowledge to glory in his mighty works, through which the physician eases pain, and the apothecary prepares his medicines, and through it, the work continues without ceasing in its efficacy on the surface of the Earth. Son, when you are ill, do not delay, but pray to Iaw, for it is he who heals.

Flee wickedness and purify your hands, cleanse your heart of every sin. Offer your sweet-smelling oblation and memorial, a generous offering according to your means. Then give the physician his place in case he leaves, and you need him too, for there are times when recovery is in his hands. He too prays to Iaw that his diagnosis is correct and his treatment brings about a cure. Whoever is a sinner before his creator will be defiant toward the physician.

Son, shed tears for one who is dead with wailing and bitter lament, as is only proper. Prepare the body and do not be absent from the burial. Weeping bitterly, mourning fully, pay your tribute of sorrow, as deserved for a day or two to prevent gossip, then compose yourself after your grief. For grief can bring on death, and heartache can sap one's strength.

When a person is carried away, sorrow is over, and the life of the poor one is terrible to the heart. Do not turn your thoughts to him again, and stop trying to remember him. Instead, think rather of the final destination. Do not remember him, for there is no hope of his return, and you do no good for him, and you harm yourself. Remember that his fate will also be yours. For him, it was yesterday, for you today. With the dead at peace, let the memories stop, and be consoled once the spirit has left.

The scribe's wisdom increases Sophia, whoever is free from struggle can become wise. How can one become learned who guides the plow, and thrills in wielding the goad like a lance? Who guides the ox and urges on the bullock, and whose every concern is for livestock?

His concern is to plow furrows, and he is careful to fatten the livestock. Likewise with every engraver and designer who labors night and day to create carved seals, and whose concern is to vary the pattern. His determination is to produce a lifelike impression, and he is careful to finish the work, so too the smith sitting by the anvil, intent on the iron he forges.

The flame from the fire sears his flesh, yet he struggles away in the furnace heat. The clang of the hammer deafens his ears, and his eyes are on the object he is shaping. His determination is to finish the work, and he is careful to perfect it in detail. Likewise, the potter sitting at his labor, turning the wheel with his feet. He is always concerned about his products and turns them out in quantity.

With his hands, he molds the clay, and with his feet softens it. His determination is to complete the glazing, and he is careful to fire the kiln. All these are skilled with their hands, each one an expert at his own work. Without them, no city could be lived in, and wherever they stay, they do not go hungry. But they are not sought after for the council of the people nor are they prominent in the assembly.

They do not sit on the judge's bench, nor can they understand law and justice. They cannot explain discipline or judgment, nor are they found among the rulers. Yet they maintain the fabric of the world, and their concern is for the exercise of their skill.

Wisdom of Joshua ben Sira: Chapter 38 Notes

1 Codex Sinaiticus: ypsistou (ΥΨΙϹΤΟΥ). Translation: highest

• Genizah manuscript B: ål yhkm (אל יחכם). Translation: god of wisdom (or wise)

The term found in Genizah manuscript B is reminiscent of the Zoroastrian God Ahura Mazda's name, which translates as Lord of Wisdom. This suggests that the Hebrew translation of the book was made in the Parthian or Sassanian empires, both of which were officially Zoroastrian, and were home to many Jews, Samaritans, and Nazarenes who fled persecution within the Roman and Byzantine empires.

Wisdom of Joshua ben Sira: Chapter 39

How different is the person who devotes himself to the study of the Orit of the Highest! He explores the wisdom of all the ancients and is occupied with the prophecies, and he preserves the discourses of the famous and goes to the heart of involved sayings. He seeks out the hidden meaning of proverbs and is busied with the enigmas found in parables.

He is in attendance on the great and appears before rulers. He travels among the peoples of foreign lands to test what is good and evil among people. His care is to rise early to seek Iaw his creator, to petition the Highest, to open his mouth in prayer, to ask pardon for his sins.

If Iaw the Great is willing, he will be filled with the spirit of understanding, he will pour out his words of wisdom and in prayer give praise to Iaw. He will direct his knowledge and his counsel, as he meditates on his mysteries. He will show the wisdom of what he has learned and glory in the Orit of the lord of the covenant.

Many will praise his understanding, and his name can never be blotted out, unfading will be his memory, and through all generations, his name will live. People will speak of his wisdom, and the assembly will declare his praise. While he lives he is one out of a thousand, and when he dies he leaves a good name.

Once more I will set out my theme to shine like the moon in its fullness! Listen to me, my faithful children, and open up your petals like roses planted near running waters. Send up the sweet odor of incense, break forth in blossoms like the lily. Raise your voices in a chorus of praise, and bless Iaw for all his works!

Proclaim the greatness of his name, loudly sing his praises, with music on the harp and all stringed instruments, and sing out with joy as you proclaim. The works of Iaw are all of them good, and he supplies for every need in its own time. At his word, the waters become still as in a flask, and he had but to speak and the reservoirs were made. He has but to command and his will is done, and nothing can limit his saving action.

The works of all humankind are present to him, and nothing is hidden from his eyes. His gaze spans all the ages. Is there any limit to his saving action? To him, nothing is small or insignificant, and nothing is too wonderful or hard for him.

No cause then to say, "What is the purpose of this?"

Everything is intended to satisfy a need, and his blessing overflows like the Nile, and like the Euphrates, it enriches the surface of the earth. Even so, his anger dispossesses the nations and turns fertile land into a salt marsh. For the virtuous, his paths are level, to the haughty they are clogged with stones.

Good things for the good he provided from the beginning, but for the wicked good things and bad. First of all, the needs for human life are water and fire, iron and salt, the heart of wheat, milk, honey, the blood of the grape, oil, and clothing. For the good all these are good, but for the wicked, they turn out evil.

There are zephyrs created to punish, and in their fury, they can dislodge mountains. In a time of destruction, they hurl their force and calm the anger of their creator. Fire and hail, famine, and disease, too were created for punishment. Ravenous beasts, scorpions, vipers, and the avenging sword to exterminate the wicked, and all these were created to meet a need, and are kept in his storehouse for the proper time.

When he commands them, they rejoice, in their assigned tasks they do not disobey his command. That is why from the first I took my stand, and wrote it down as my theme. The works of Iaw are all of them good, he supplies for every need in its own time. There is no cause then to say, "This is not as good as that," for each shows its worth at the proper time. So now with full heart and voice proclaim and bless the name Iaw!

Wisdom of Joshua ben Sira: Chapter 40

Great labor was created for every man, and a heavy yoke to the children of Adam, from the day they leave their mother's womb until the day they return to the mother of all the living. Troubled thoughts and fear of heart are theirs and anxious foreboding until death. Whether one sits on a lofty throne or grovels in dust and ashes, whether one wears a splendid crown or is clothed in the coarsest of garments.

There are anger and envy, trouble and dread, the terror of death, fury, and strife. Even when one lies on his bed to rest, his cares disturb his sleep at night. So short is his rest that it seems like none, until in his dreams he struggles as he did by day, and is troubled by the visions of his mind, like a fugitive fleeing from the pursuer.

As he reaches safety, he wakes up, astonished that there is nothing to fear. To all flesh, human being, and beast, but for sinners, seven times more, come plague and bloodshed, fiery heat and drought, plunder and ruin, famine and death. For the wicked evil was created, and because of them, destruction rushes.

All that is of earth returns to earth, and what is from above returns above. All that comes from bribes or injustice will be wiped out, but loyalty remains forever. Wealth from injustice is like an overflowing river, like a mighty stream with lightning and thunder, which, in its rising, rolls along the stones, but suddenly, once and for all, comes to an end.

The offshoot of violence will not flourish, for the source of the godless is on sheer rock. They are like reeds on riverbanks, withered before all other plants, but goodness, like an eternity, will never be cut off, and righteousness endures forever. Wealth or wages can make life sweet, but better than either is finding a treasure.

A child or a city will preserve one's name, but better than either is finding Sophia. Livestock and orchards make a person flourish, but better than either is a devoted wife. Wine and strong drink delight the mind, but better than either is the love of friends. Flute and harp offer a sweet melody, but better than either is a pure tongue. Grace and beauty delight the eye, but better than either is the produce of the field.

A friend and a neighbor are timely guides, but better than either is a sensible wife. Relatives and helpers for times of stress, but better than either is the charity that rescues. Gold and silver make one's way secure, but better than either is sound judgment. Wealth and vigor make the heart exult, but better than either is fear of Iaw. In revering Iaw there is no need, whoever has it needs to seek no other support. Revering Iaw is a paradise of blessings, and its canopy is over all that is glorious.

Son, do not live the life of a beggar, it is better to die than to beg. When one has to look at a stranger's table, life is not worth living. The delicacies offered to bring revulsion of spirit and to the intelligent, inward torture. In the mouth of the shameless begging is sweet, but within him, it burns like fire.

Wisdom of Joshua ben Sira: Chapter 41

Oh, Mot![1] How bitter is the thought of you for the one at peace in his home? For the one who is serene and always successful, who can still enjoy life's pleasures.

Oh, Mot! How welcome is your sentence to the weak, failing in strength, stumbling and tripping on everything, with sight gone and hope lost. Do not fear death's decree for you, and remember, it embraces those before you and those to come. This decree for all flesh, and why then should you reject the decree of the Highest?

Whether life was ten or a hundred or a thousand years, there is no debate regarding Sheol. The children of sinners are a degenerate line, and stupid offspring are from the homes of the wicked. The inheritance of children of sinners will perish, and on their offspring will be a perpetual disgrace.

Children curse their wicked father, for they allow disgrace because of him. Curses on you wicked people who ignore the Orit of the Highest. If you have children, calamity will be theirs, and if you father them, it will be only for groaning. When you stumble, there is lasting joy, and when you die, you become a curse.

All that is nothing returns to nothing, and so too the unjust from void to void. The human body is a fleeting thing, but a virtuous name will never be annihilated. Have respect for your name, for it will stand by you more than thousands of precious treasures. The good things of life last a number of days, but a good name, for days without number.

Hidden wisdom and concealed treasure, of what value is either? Better is the person who hides his foolishness than the one who hides his wisdom. My children, listen to the instruction about shame and judge disgrace according to my rules, and not every kind of shame is shameful or is every kind of disgrace to be recognized.

Before father and mother, be ashamed of immorality.

Before the prince and ruler, be ashamed of falsehood.

Before master and mistress, be ashamed of deceit.

Before the public assembly, be ashamed of crime.

Before associates and friends, be ashamed of disloyalty.

In the place where you live, be ashamed of theft.

Be ashamed of breaking an oath or a covenant, and of stretching your elbow at dinner, of refusing to give when asked, of rebuffing your own relatives, of defrauding another of his appointed share, of failing to return a greeting, of looking at a man's wife and entertaining thoughts about another woman, of trifling with a servant girl you have, of violating her bed, of using harsh words with friends, and of following up your gifts with insults.

Wisdom of Joshua ben Sira: Chapter 41 Notes

1 Codex Sinaiticus: Thanate (ΘΑΝΑΤΕ). Translation: Thanatos (or death)

• Genizah manuscript B: Mût (מות). Translation: Mot (or death)

The Hebrew word mût (מות) is generally assumed to be a spelling error of mû̆ût (מוות), meaning "death," however, as the Hebrew (Assyrian Block Letter form of Aramaic) script did not exist in the time of Joshua, it must be assumed that the earlier Phoenician or Aramaic script was originally used to compose his book of wisdom. Mot, spelled variously as mūtu (𒄷) in Akkadian cuneiform, mt (𓅓𓏇) in Egyptian, mata (𓈖𓏇) in Kushite, mt (𐎐𐎚) in Ugaritic, mt (𐤌𐤕) in Phoenician, mût (𐡌𐡅𐡕) in Aramaic, mmt (ⵎⵎⵜ) in Tamazight, mûta (ܡܘܬܐ) in Syriac, mout (ⲙⲟⲩⲧ) in Coptic, mata (𐦨𐦷) in Meroitic, mawt (موت) in Arabic, and mot (ሞት) in Ge'ez, was the word for death, as well as the god of death in Canaan. In the Israelite texts, Mot was treated like the angel of death, instead of the god of death. Mot is well documented among the Canaanite gods in the Ugaritic Texts and the writings of Sanchuniathon, both dated to the 2nd millennium BC. In the Canaanite religion, Mot was the son of El (God), and the ruler of the "pit" called Mirey, where the dead resided.

Wisdom of Joshua ben Sira: Chapter 42

[Be ashamed] of repeating what you hear, or of betraying any secret. Be ashamed of the right things, and you will find favor in the sight of all, but of these things do not be ashamed, in case you sin to save face:

Of the Orit of the Highest and his precepts, or of justice that acquits the unjust.

Of sharing the expenses of a business or a journey, or of dividing an inheritance or property.

Of the accuracy of scales and balances, and tested measures and weights.

Of acquiring much or little, or of bargaining in dealing with a merchant.

Of constant training of children, or of beating the sides of a wicked servant;

Of a seal to keep a foolish wife at home, or of a key where there are many hands.

Of numbering every deposit, or of recording all that is taken in and given out.

Of chastisement for the silly and the foolish, or the aged and infirm answering for unrestrained conduct.

By doing so you will be truly refined and recognized by all as discreet. A daughter is a treasure that keeps her father wakeful and worries about her drives away sleep. In her youth when she remains unmarried, when she is married that she remains childless, while unmarried in case she is raped, or in her husband's house if she should prove unfaithful. Whether she becomes pregnant in her father's house or is sterile in her husband's house.

Son, keep a close watch on your daughter, in case she makes you a laughingstock for your enemies, an insult in the city and the assembly of the people, and an object of derision in public gatherings. See that there is no window in her room or spot that overlooks the approach to the house. Do not let her reveal her beauty to any male, or spend her time with married women, for just as moths come from garments, so a woman's wickedness comes from a woman. Better is a man's harshness than a woman's indulgence or a frightened daughter than any embarrassment.

Now will I describe Iaw's works, I will describe what I have seen. By Iaw's words, his works were brought into being, and he accepted the one who does his will. The sun looks down on everything with his light, and the work of Iaw is full of his glory, yet even Iaws's holy ones must fail in recounting the wonders of Iaw, which Iaw the almighty has given his forces the strength to stand firm before his glory. He searches out the abyss and penetrates the heart and their secrets he understands. For the Highest possesses all knowledge, and sees from of old the things that are to come. He makes known the past and the future and reveals the deepest secrets.

He lacks no understanding, and nothing escapes him. He regulates the mighty deeds of Sophia. He is from all eternity one and the same, with nothing added, nothing taken away, and no need for a counselor!

How beautiful are all his works, delightful to gaze on, and a joy to see! Everything lives and remains forever, and to meet each need all things are preserved. All of them differ, one from another, yet none of them has he made in vain, for each in turn, as it comes, is good, can one ever see enough of their splendor?

Wisdom of Joshua ben Sira: Chapter 43

The beauty of the celestial heights and the pure firmament, and the sky itself manifests its glory.

The sun at its rising shines at its fullest, a wonderful instrument, the work of the Highest! At noon it scorches the earth, and who can bear its fiery heat? Like a blazing furnace of solid metal, the sun's rays burn the mountains three times as much. Its fiery tongue consumes the world, and its eyes are burned by its fire. The great Iaw made it, and at whose orders it speeds on its course.

It is the moon that marks the changing seasons, governing the times, their lasting sign. By it, we know the sacred seasons and pilgrimage feasts, a light that wanes in its course. The month is called after her name, increasing wonderfully in her changing. A military signal for the forces above, it lights the firmament with its brilliance, and the beauty of the skies and the glory of the stars, a shining ornament in the heights of Iaw. By the command of Qetesh, the moon keeps its appointed place and does not fade as the stars keep watch.

See the rainbow! Then bless its creator for majestic indeed is its splendor. It spans the skies with its glory, the hand of the Highest has stretched it out in power. His rebuke marks out the path for the hail and makes the lightning of his judgment shine forth. For his own purposes, he opens the storehouse and makes the rain clouds fly like vultures.

His might gives the clouds their strength and breaks off the hailstones. The thunder of his voice makes the earth shake, and by his power, he shakes the mountains. A word from him drives on the south wind, whirlwind, hurricane, and tornado. He makes the snow fly like birds, and it settles down like swarms of locusts.

Its shining whiteness blinds the eyes, the mind marvels at its steady fall. He scatters frost like salt, and it shines like flowers on the rosebush. He sends cold northern blasts that harden the ponds like solid ground, spread a crust over every body of water, and clothes each pool with a coat of armor.

When mountain growth is scorched by heat, and flowering plains as by fire, and the dripping clouds restore them all, and the scattered dew enriches the parched land. His is the plan that calms the deep and plants the islands in the sea. Those who go down to the sea recount its extent, and when we hear them we are thunderstruck. In it are his creatures, stupendous, amazing, all kinds of life, and the monsters of the deep.

For him, each messenger succeeds, and at his bidding accomplishes his will. More than this we need not add, and let the last word be, he is the all! Let us praise him all the more since we cannot fathom him, for greater is he than all his works. Awesome indeed is Iaw, and wonderful his power.

Raise your voices to glorify Iaw as much as you can, for there is still more. Praise him with renewed strength, do not grow weary, for you cannot fathom him. For who has seen him and can describe him? Who can praise him as he is? Beyond these, many things lie hidden, only a few of his works have I seen. It is the Lord who has made all things, and to those who fear him, he gives Sophia.

Wisdom of Joshua ben Sira: Chapter 44

I will now praise the just, our ancestors, in their own time, the abounding glory of the Lord's portion, his own part, since the days of old. Heroes of the land, in kingly fashion, renowned for their might, counselors in their prudence, seers of all things in prophecy, resolute princes of the flock, lawgivers and their laws, sages skilled in composition, authors of sharp proverbs, composers of melodious psalms, writers of lyric poems.

Loyal, solidly established, and at peace in their own estates. All these were glorious in their time, illustrious in their day. Some of them left behind a name so that people recount their praises. Of others, no memory remains, for when they perished, they perished, as if they had never lived, they and their children after them. Yet these also were just, and their virtues have not been forgotten.

Their wealth remains in their families, their heritage with their descendants. Through God's covenant their family endures, and their offspring for their sake.

For all time their progeny will endure, their glory will never be blotted out, their bodies are buried in peace, but their name lives on and on. At gatherings, their wisdom is retold, and the assembly proclaims their praises.

Enoch walked with Iaw and was taken up, so succeeding generations might learn by his example.

Noah, found just and perfect, renewed the race in the time of devastation, because of his value there were survivors, and with a sign to him, the deluge ended. A lasting covenant was made with him, that never again would all flesh be destroyed.

Abraham, father of many peoples, kept his glory without stain, he observed the Highest's command and entered into a covenant with him, and in his own flesh he incised the ordinance, and when tested was found loyal. For this reason, God promised him with an oath to bless the nations through his descendants, to make him numerous as grains of dust, and to exalt his descendants like the stars.

Giving them an inheritance from sea to sea, and from the river to the ends of the earth. For Isaac, too, he renewed the same promise because of Abraham, his father. The covenant with all his ancestors was confirmed, and the blessing rested on the head of Israel. Iaw acknowledged him as the firstborn and gave him his inheritance. He fixed the boundaries for his tribes and their division into twelve.

Wisdom of Joshua ben Sira: Chapter 45

From him came the man who would win the favor of all the living, dear to Iaw and human beings: Moses, whose memory is a blessing. Iaw made him equal to the messengers in honor and strengthened him with fearful powers. At his words, Iaw performed signs and sustained him in the king's presence. He gave him the command-ments for his people and revealed to him his glory. Because of his trustworthiness and meekness, Iaw selected him from all flesh. He let him hear his voice and led him into the cloud, where he handed over the commandments, the law of life and understanding, that he might teach his rules to Jacob, and his judgments and decrees to Israel.

Like Moses, he also raised up his brother Aaron of the tribe of Levi. He made his office perpetual and bestowed on him priesthood for his people. He established him in honor and crowned him with lofty majesty. He clothed him in splendid garments and adorned him with glorious clothes, pants, tunic, and robe with pomegranates at the hem, and a rustle of bells around, whose pleasing sound at each step would make him heard within the sanctuary, a reminder for the people.

The sacred vestments of gold, violet, and crimson, worked with embroidery, and the breastplate for the decision, the vest and cincture with scarlet yarn, the work of the weaver, and precious stones with seal engravings in golden settings, the work of the jeweler, and to commemorate in incised letters each of the tribes of Israel. On his turban was a diadem of gold, its plate engraved with the sacred inscription. Majestic, glorious, renowned for splendor, a delight to the eyes, supremely beautiful.

Before him, no one had been adorned with these, and neither may they ever be worn by any other except his descendants alone, generation after generation, for all time. His grain offering is wholly burnt as an established offering twice each day. Moses ordained him and anointed him with the holy oil, in a lasting covenant with him and his family, as permanent as the skies, that he should serve Iaw in the priesthood and bless the people in his name.

He chose him from all the living to sacrifice burnt offerings and choice portions, to burn incense, sweet odor as a memorial, and to atone for the people of Israel. He gave to him the laws, and authority to prescribe and to judge. To teach precepts to the people, and judgments to the Israelites.

Foreigners rose in anger against him, and grew jealous of him in the desert, the followers of Dathan and Abiram, and the band of Korah in their defiance. When

Iaw saw this he became angry and destroyed them in his burning anger. He brought against them a marvel and consumed them in flaming fire. Then he increased the glory of Aaron and bestowed on him his inheritance. The sacred offerings he allotted to him, with the show-bread as his portion. The oblations of Iaw are his food, a gift to him, and his descendants, but he holds no land among the people or shares with them their heritage, for Iaw himself is his portion and inheritance among the Israelites.

Phineas too, the son of Eleazar, was the courageous third of his line when zealous for the god of all, he met the crisis of his people and, at the prompting of his noble heart, atoned for the Israelites. Therefore, on him also God conferred the right, in a covenant of friendship, to provide for the sanctuary, so that he and his descendants should possess the high priesthood forever.

For even his covenant with David, the son of Jesse of the tribe of Judah was an individual heritage through one son alone, but the heritage of Aaron is for all his descendants.

So now bless Iaw who has crowned you with glory! May he grant you the wisdom of heart to govern his people in justice, in case the benefits you confer should be forgotten, or your authority, throughout all time.

Wisdom of Joshua ben Sira: Chapter 46

Joshua the son of Nun, the aide to Moses in the prophetic office was a valiant warrior, formed to be, as his name implies, the great savior of Iaw's chosen ones, to punish the enemy and to give to Israel their heritage. What glory was his when he raised his hand, to brandish his sword against the city! Who could withstand him when he fought the battles of Iaw?

Was it not by that same hand the sun stopped so that one day became two? He called on the Highest God when his enemies surrounded him, and the Highest god answered him with hailstones of tremendous power that rained down on the hostile army on the hill until he destroyed the enemy, so all the doomed nations might know Iaw was watching over his people's battles.

He was a devoted follower of Iaw and showed himself loyal in Moses' lifetime. He and Caleb, son of Jephunneh, when they opposed the rebel assembly, averted Iaw's anger from the people and suppressed the wicked complaint. Because of this, these two alone were spared from the six hundred thousand infantry, to lead the people into their heritage, the land flowing with milk and honey.

The strength the Lord gave to Caleb remained with him even in old age until he won his way onto the summits of the land, his family too received a heritage, that all the offspring of Jacob might know how good it is to be a devoted follower of Iaw. The Judges, each one of them, whose hearts were not deceived, who did not abandon Iaw may their memory be ever blessed! May their bones flourish with a new life where they lie, and their names receive fresh luster in their children!

Beloved of his people, dear to his creator, pledged in a vow from his mother's womb, as one consecrated to Iaw in the prophetic office, was Samuel, the judge who offered sacrifice. At Iaw's command, he established the kingdom and annointed princes to rule the people. Through the Orit of Iaw, he judged the congregation and visited the encampments of Jacob. As a trustworthy prophet, he was seached for and his words proved him to be a true seer.

He, too, called on Lord Sabaoth when his enemies pressed him on every side and offered up a suckling lamb. Then Iaw thundered from the sky, and the tremendous roar of his voice was heard. He brought low the rulers of the enemy and destroyed all the lords of the Gentiles. When Samuel neared the end of life, he testified before Iaw and his anointed prince, "No bribe or secret gift have I taken from anyone!" and no one could accuse him. Even after death, his guidance was wanted, and he made known to the king his fate. From the grave, he spoke prophecy to put an end to wickedness.

Wisdom of Joshua ben Sira: Chapter 47

After him came Nathan, who served in David's presence. Like the choice fat of sacred offerings, so was David in Israel. He played with lions as though they were young goats and with bears, like lambs of the flock. As a youth, he struck down the giant and wiped out the people's disgrace. His hand slung the stone that shattered the pride of Goliath. For he had called on the Highest God, who gave strength to his right arm to defeat the skilled warrior and establish the might of his people. Therefore the women sang his praises and honored him for "the tens of thousands." When he received the royal crown, he battled and conquered the enemies on all sides. He campaigned against the hostile Pelesets[1] and shattered their power until our own day.

With his every deed he offered thanks to Iaw the Highest, in words of praise. With his whole heart, he loved his creator and daily had his praises sung, and he added beauty to the feasts and celebrated the seasons of each year with string music before the altar, providing sweet melody for the psalms so that when the Qetesh's name was praised, before daybreak the sanctuary would resound.

Iaw forgave him for his sins and praised his strength forever. He conferred on him the rights of royalty and established his throne in Israel. Because of his merits, he had as a successor a wise son, who lived in security.

Solomon reigned during an era of peace for God brought rest to all his borders. He built a temple in the name of Iaw and established an eternal sanctuary. How wise you were when you were young, overflowing with instruction, like a flooding river!

Your understanding covered the whole earth, and, like a sea, filled it with knowledge. Your fame reached distant coasts, and you were beloved for your peaceful reign. With song and proverb and riddle, and with your answers, you astounded the nations. By the name of the god Iaw, who is called the god of Israel. Gold you gathered like so much iron, you heaped up silver as though it were lead. But you abandoned yourself to women and gave them dominion over your body.

You brought a stain on your glory, shame on your marriage bed, anger on your descendants, and groaning on your deathbed, and so two governments came into being when in Ephraim kingship was usurped. Yet the Lord did not withdraw his mercy, nor permit even one of his promises to fail. He does not uproot the posterity of the chosen or destroy the offspring of his friends.

So he gave to Jacob a remnant, to David a source from his own family. Solomon finally slept with his ancestors and left behind him one of his sons, broad in foolishness, narrow in sense, whose policy made the people rebel. Then arose the one who should not be remembered, the sinner who led Israel into sin, who brought ruin to Ephraim and caused them to be exiled from their land. Their sinfulness grew more and more, and they gave themselves to every evil.

Wisdom of Joshua ben Sira: Chapter 47 Notes

1 Codex Sinaiticus: Phylistiim (ΦΥΛΙϹΤΙΙΜ). Translation: Pelesets (or Palestinians)

• Genizah manuscript B: plštym (פלשתים). Translation: Pelesets (or Palestinians)

The Pelesets were an ancient people based in the region of the modern Gaza Strip of the Palestinian Territories. The earliest surviving mention of them is from the reliefs of the Temple of Ramses III at Medinet Habu in Egypt that dates back to some time between 1186 and 1155 BC, in which they were called Půlåsåtî ([illegible]). It is unclear where they came from, however, one theory is that they were the Pala, a Luwian people from the Black Sea coast of Anatolia. The region was an independent country called Palaa (𒉺𒆷𒀀) in the Hittite records from the 1600s BC, however, had become part of the Nesite Empire by the 1500s BC. Around the time the Pelesets invaded Canaan, the Pala were driven from their homeland by the neighboring Kaskians from northeast Anatolia, which supports the connection between the groups, however, it has yet to be proven conclusively. They were reported to have been taken as captives by the Babylonians and resettled in Mesopotamia in 604 BC.

Wisdom of Joshua ben Sira: Chapter 48

Then like fire the prophet Elijah appeared, his words a flaming furnace. The staff of life, their bread, he shattered, and in his zeal, he made them few in number. Through God's words, he closed up the skies and three times brought down fire. How awesome are you, Elijah!

Whose glory is equal to yours? You brought a dead body back to life from Sheol, by the will of the Highest. You sent kings down to destruction, and nobles, from their beds of sickness. You heard threats at Sinai, and at Horeb avenging judgments. You anointed the agent of these punishments, the prophet to succeed in your place.

You were taken aloft in a whirlwind, in a chariot with fiery horses. You are destined, it is inscribed to reproof the weather before it breaks out in fury, and to turn back the hearts of parents toward their children, and to re-establish the tribes of Jacob. Blessed is the one who will have seen you before he dies!

When Elijah was enveloped in the whirlwind, Elisha was filled with his spirit, and he worked twice as many marvels, and every utterance of his mouth was wonderful. During his lifetime he was afraid of no one, nor was anyone able to intimidate his will. Nothing was beyond his power, and from where he lay buried, his body prophesied. In life, he performed wonders, and after death, marvelous deeds. Despite all this, the people did not repent or did they give up their sins until they were uprooted from their land and scattered all over the earth. Yet Judah remained a tiny people, with its ruler from the house of David. Some of them did what was right, but others were extremely sinful.

Hezekiah fortified his city and had water brought into it, with bronze tools he cut through the rocks and dammed up a mountain site for water. During his reign, Sennacherib led an invasion and sent his adjutant, and he shook his fist at Zion and blasphemed in his pride.

The people's hearts melted within them, and they were in anguish like that of childbirth, but they called upon the Lord who is merciful, spreading forth their hands toward him, and Qetesh and lifted their hands to her, and he heard the prayer they spoke and saved them through Isaiah. He struck the camp of the Assyrians and routed them with a plague.

For Hezekiah did what was right and held fast to the paths of David, as ordered by the illustrious prophet Isaiah, who saw the truth in visions. In his lifetime he turned back the sun and prolonged the life of the king. By his powerful spirit, he looked into the future and consoled the mourners of Zion, he foretold what would happen till the end of time, hidden things yet to be fulfilled.

Wisdom of Joshua ben Sira: Chapter 49

The name Josiah is like blended incense made lasting by a skilled perfumer. Precious is his memory, like honey to the taste, like music at a banquet. For he grieved over our betrayals and destroyed the abominable idols. He kept his heart fixed on Iaw and in times of lawlessness practiced virtue.

Except for David, Hezekiah, and Josiah, they all were wicked, they abandoned the Law of the Highest, these kings of Judah, right to the very end. So he gave over their power to others, their glory to a foreign nation who burned the holy city and left its streets desolate, as foretold by Jeremiah. They mistreated him who even in the womb had been made a prophet, to source out, pull down, and destroy, and then to build and to plant.

Ezekiel saw a vision and described the different creatures of the chariot, he also referred to Job, who always persevered in the right path. Then, too, the Twelve Prophets, may their bones flourish with a new life where they lie! They gave new strength to Jacob and saved him with steadfast hope.

How to praise Zerubbabel? He was like a signet ring on the right hand.

Jeshua ben Jehozadak? In their time they rebuilt the altar and erected the holy temple, destined for everlasting glory.

Praised be the memory of Nehemiah! He rebuilt our ruined walls and restored our shattered defenses, and set up gates and bars.

Few on earth have been created like Enoch, he also was taken up in his body.

Was ever a man born like Joseph? Even his dead body was provided for.

Glorious, too, were Shem and Seth and Enosh, but beyond that of any living being was the splendor of Adam.

Wisdom of Joshua ben Sira: Chapter 50

The greatest of his family, the glory of his people, was Simeon the son of Onias, the high priest, in whose time the temple of Iaw was renovated, in whose days the temple was reinforced. In his time also the retaining wall was built with powerful turrets for the temple precincts. In his time the reservoir was dug, a pool as vast as the sea.

He protected the people against brigands and strengthened the city against the enemy. How splendid he was as he looked out from the tent, as he came from behind the veil! Like a star shining among the clouds, like the full moon at the festal season, and like the sun shining on the temple of the king, like a rainbow appearing in the cloudy sky, like flowers on the branches in springtime, like a lily by running waters, like a green shoot on Lebanon in summer, as the fire of incense at a sacrifice.

Like a vessel of hammered gold, studded with all kinds of precious stones, like a luxuriant olive tree heavy with fruit, a plant with branches abounding in oil, wearing his glorious robes, and vested in sublime magnificence, as he ascended the glorious altar and lent majesty to the court of the sanctuary.

When he received the portions from the priests while he stood before the sacrificial wood, his sons stood around him like a garland, like young cedars on Lebanon, like poplars by the brook they surrounded him, all the sons of Aaron in their glory, with the offerings to Iaw in their hands, in the presence of the whole assembly of Israel.

Once he had completed the service at the altar and arranged the sacrificial hearth for the Highest, had stretched forth his hand for the cup, to offer the blood of the grape, and poured it out at the foot of the altar, a sweet-smelling odor to the Highest God. Then the sons of Aaron would sound a blast, the priests, on their trum-pets of beaten metal, a blast to resound mightily as a reminder before the Highest.

All the people with one accord would fall with face to the ground in adoration before the Highest, before the Holy One of Israel. Then hymns would re-echo, and over the throng sweet strains of praise resound. All the people of the land would shout for joy, praying to the Merciful One, as the high priest completed the service at the altar by presenting to God the fitting sacrifice.

Then coming down he would raise his hands over all the congregation of Israel, the blessing of Iaw would be on his lips, and the name of Iaw would be his glory. The people would again fall down to receive the blessing of the Highest. Now, bless the God of all, who has done wonders on earth, who fosters growth from the womb, fashioning it according to his will!

May he grant you a wise heart and abide with you in peace. May his goodness toward Simeon last forever, and may he fulfill for him the covenant with Phineas so that it may not be abrogated for him or his descendants while the skies last. I hate two nations, and a third is not even a people: The Samarians[1] and Pelesets, and the foolish people who live in Shechem.[2]

Wise instruction, appropriate proverbs, I have written in this book, I, Joshua ben Sira ben Eleazar (the Jerusalemite,)[3] as they poured out from my heart's understanding. Happy those who meditate on these things. Wise are those who take them to heart! If they put them into practice, they can cope with anything, for the light of Iaw is their lamp.

Wisdom of Joshua ben Sira: Chapter 50 Notes

1 Codex Sinaiticus: Samarias (ϲΑΜΑΡΕΙΑϲ). Translation: Samaritans

• Genizah manuscript B: yûšby šôyr (ישבי שעיר).

Translation: inhabitants of Seir

The Greek and Hebrew translations do not refer to the same location, as Mount Seir was in Edom, modern Jordan, while Samaria was in the modern Palestinian West Bank. Most scholars have accepted that "Samaritan" was a mistranslation since the Genizah manuscripts were published, as Shechem, which is mentioned at the end of the list, is in Samaria, and there is no reason to list them as two separate peoples. However, Joshua did state that the third group was not a people, which suggests the "foolish people in Shechem" was a reference to the Samaritan priesthood, which was based in Shechem.

The Jews in the time of the Second Temple Era did not accept the Samaritans as being descendants of the ancient Samaritans, but instead accepted Ezra the scribe's claim that they were Babylonians who settled in Judea during Babylonian rule. This continues to be the Rabbinical Jewish opinion on Samaritans, and the State of Israel continues to classify them as Palestinians.

It is not clear when "Samaritan" would have been replaced with "inhabitants of Seir," however, was most likely sometime between 70 and 550 AD, when the Samaritans were the largest of the Israelite religions in Roman and then Byzantine Palestine.

2 Codex Sinaiticus: Sicimois (ⲥⲓⲕⲓⲙⲟⲓⲥ). Translation: Shechem

• Genizah manuscript B: škm (שכם). Translation: Shechem

This reference to a third group besides the Samarians and Pelesets in Judea, who are not large enough to be considered a people, implies the Samaritan priesthood, which was based in Shechem at the time.

3 Codex Sinaiticus: Iêsous huios Sirach Eleazar ho Ierosolymitês (ⲓⲏⲥⲟⲩⲥ ⲩⲓⲟⲥ ⲥⲓⲣⲁⲭ ⲉⲗⲉⲁⲍⲁⲣ ⲟ ιερΟϹΟΛΥΜΙΤΗϹ). Translation: Jesus (or Joshua) son of Sira Eleazar the Jerusalemite

• Genizah manuscript B: yšûô bn âlôzr bn syrå (ישוע בן אלעזר בן סירא). Translation: Yehua (or Joshua) ben Eleazar ben Sira.

The sentence ends in Genizah manuscript B without mentioning he was a Jerusalemite, suggesting the translator added this, and so it is treated as a scribal note. The transliteration "Sirach" was often seen in older Christian translations, however, the Aramaic and Hebrew name was Sira, which is restored in this translation, as it is in most modern English translations.

Wisdom of Joshua ben Sira: Chapter 51

I thank you, Lord King,[1] I praise you, God my savior! I proclaim your name, refuge of my life, because you have ransomed my life from death, and you held back my body from the pit and delivered my foot from the power of Sheol. You have preserved me from the scourge of the slanderous tongue, and from the lips of those who went over to falsehood.

You were with me against those who rise up against me, and you have rescued me according to your abundant mercy from the snare of those who look for my downfall, and from the power of those who seek my life. From many dangers, you have saved me, from flames that beset me on every side, from the middle of fire till there was not a whiff of it, from the deep belly of Sheol, from deceiving lips and painters of lies, from the arrows of a treacherous tongue.

I was at the point of death, my life was nearing the depths of Sheol, and I turned every way, but there was no one to help, and I looked for support but there was none. Then I remembered the mercies of Iaw, his acts of kindness through ages past, for he saves those who take refuge in him, and rescues them from every evil.

So I raised my voice from the grave, from the gates of Sheol I cried for help. I called out, "Iaw the father of my lord,[2] don't abandon me in times of trouble, among storms and dangers. I will always praise your name and remember you in prayer!"

Then Iaw heard my voice and listened to my appeal. He saved me from every evil and preserved me in times of trouble. For this reason, I thank and praise him, and I bless the name Iaw. When I was young and innocent, I searched for Sophia. Before the temple, I asked for her, and until the end, I will search for her.

As the flowers yielded to ripening grapes, the heart's joy and my feet kept to the level path because from the earliest youth, I was familiar with her. In a short time, I paid attention, I met with great instruction. Since in this way I have benefited, I will give my teacher grateful praise. I resolved to tread her path, and I have been jealous of the good and will not turn back.

I burned with desire for her, never relenting. I became preoccupied with her, never weary of extolling her. I spread out my hands to the skies and I came to know her secrets. For her I purified my hands, in cleanness I attained to her.

At first acquaintance with her, I gained an understanding such that I will never ignore her. My whole being was stirred to seek her, and therefore I have made her my prize possession. Iaw has rewarded me with a tongue, with it I praise him.[3] Come aside to me, you untutored, and take up lodging in the house of instruction. How long will you deprive yourself of wisdom's food, how long endure such bitter thirst?

I open my mouth and speak of her, gain wisdom for yourselves at no cost. Take her yoke on your neck, so your mind may receive her teaching. For she is close to those who seek her, and the one who is in earnest finds her. See for yourselves! I have labored only a little, but have found much. Acquire but a little instruction, and you will win silver and gold through her. May your mind rejoice in his mercy, do not be ashamed to give him praise. Work at your tasks in due season, and in his own time, Iaw will give you your reward.

Wisdom of Joshua ben Sira: Chapter 51 Notes

1 Codex Sinaiticus: cyrie basileu (ⲔⲨⲢⲓⲉⲃⲁⲥⲓⲗⲉⲨ).
Translation: Lord King

• Genizah manuscript B: šmk môûz ḥyy (שמך מעוז חיי).

Translation: name of Moûz (or strong) life

The word môûz (מעוז) is an obscure religious term for 'strong' in Hebrew. It does not appear to be a Semitic or Egyptian word and its etymology is unclear. A similar term, Môzym / Ma'uzzim (מעזים / מָעֻזִּים) is used in Daniel chapter 11 (Theodotion's chapter structure) to refer to a "false god" worshiped at the temple in Jerusalem, translated as Maôzin (Μαωζιν) in Theodotion's translation. The Hebrew name in

Daniel appears to have been transliterated from the Greek word Mazaeon (Μαζαιον), the accusative declension of the Greek name Mazaeos (Μαζαιος). Mazaeos was the Greek form of Persian and Aramaic name Mzdy (מזדי), which was itself Aramaic and Persian form of the Avesta name Mazdā (مَزْدا6), meaning the god in question was Ahura Mazda, the Zoroastrian god. However, the term surviving in Masoretic Daniel does not read Mzdy (מזדי / מזדי), the Aramaic version of the name, indicating this chapter was written in Greek and then translated into Hebrew. It was most likely written by the High Priest Jaddua as Alexander the Great's armies were marching south through Canaan.

Whatever the origin of the term Maoz, the rest of the term was not in the Greek translation of the Wisdom of Joshua ben Sira, indicating that the term was not in the text he was translating. The term "Lord King" (Κύριε Βασιλευ), probably originated in the Aramaic term ådn mlkå (אדן מלכא), meaning "Lord of kings." The term would have been spelled as ådůn mlk (אדון מלך) in Hebrew, which would have appeared to be the name of the god that had been banned by King Josiah in circa 625 BC, which the Hebrew translator would have needed to replace with something.

2 Codex Sinaiticus: Cyrion patera cyriou mou (ΚΥΡΙΟΝ ΠΑΤΕΡΑΚΥΡΙΟΥΜΟΥ). Translation: Lord father of my lord
• Genizah manuscript B: yyy åby åth- (-ייי אבי אתה). Translation: Yhů father you are-

The Hebrew translation in Genizah manuscript B is very similar to the Greek translation in the Septuagint, other than the names Iaw being replaced with Cyrion and Yhů being replaced with yyy, and the end of the phrase being missing in the Hebrew translation due to damage to the manuscript.

3 Codex Sinaiticus: edôcen cyrios glôssan moe misthon mou, cae en autê aenesô auton (ЄΔѠϪΚЄΝ ΚΥΡΙΟϹ ΓΛѠϹϹΑΝ ΜΟΙ ΜΙϹΘΟΝ ΜΟΥ ΚΑΙ ЄΝ ΑΥΤΗ ΑΙΝЄϹѠ ΑΥΤΟΝ). Translation: gave Lord tongue of mine payment (or salary) of mine, and in this I praise him (or it)

• The Great Psalms Scroll: ydy prš - môrmyh åtbůnn (ויי פרש-בעירביה אתבונן). This is reconstructed as ydy prš[ty ů]môrmyh åtbůnn (ידי פרש[תי ו]מערמיה אתבונן). Translation: I will seperat[e a]rms of mine in worship

The Hebrew version of the text found at the end of The Great Psalms Scroll may, or may not be a version of chapter 51. There are damaged parallels of verses 13 to 23 and 30, but none of which are identical to the Greek translation. All references to the words "God," "Lord," or the name Yhůh are missing, suggesting this section of text was redacted after the Greek translation was made. The alternate interpretation is that this is a lost Psalm, which Joshua ben Sira, or someone before him expanded.

This verse is almost complete in the text. The previous verse is complete, but also shorter than the Greek translation, and the beginning of the next verse also survives, proving it was much shorter than the Greek version and missing the reference to the Lord.

Odes: Chapter 1

Song of Moses in Exodus

Sing of the Lord[1] who has gloriously thrown the horse and rider into the sea!

[2]My assistant and protector in my salvation. This is my God and I will glorify him, my father's God, and I will praise him."

The Lord bringing wars to nothing, Lord is his name.[3]

He has thrown the chariots of Pharaoh and his army into the sea, the chosen mounted captains! They were swallowed up in the Papyrus Sea.[4] He covered them with the sea. They sank to the depth like a stone.

Your right hand, God! Has been glorified in strength. Your right hand, God! Has broken the enemies.

In the abundance of your glory, you have broken the adversaries to pieces. You sent out your anger, and it devoured them like stubble. By the breath of your anger, the water parted asunder, the waters congealed like a wall, and the waves were congealed in the middle of the sea. The enemy said, 'I will pursue, I will overtake, I will divide the plunder. I will satisfy my mind! I will destroy with my sword, and my hand will have dominion!' You sent out your wind, and the sea covered them. They sank like lead in the mighty water.

Who is like you among the gods, Lord? Who is like you? Glorified in holiness, marvelous in glories, doing wonders. You stretched out your right hand, and Eretz[5] swallowed them up. You have guided in your righteousness this your people whom you have redeemed, by your strength you have called them into your holy resting place. The nations heard and were angry, pangs seized the residents among the Gentiles. Then, the princes of Edom and the chiefs of the Moabites ran as trembling took hold of them, and all the inhabitants of Canaan melted away.

Let trembling and fear fall on them. By the greatness of your arm, let them become like a stone until your people pass over, Lord! Until these, your people pass over, who you purchased. Bring them in and plant them in the mountain of their inheritance, in your prepared habitation, which you, Lord, have prepared, the sanctuary of the Lord, which your hands have prepared. Lord, reigning forever and ever and ever. For the horse of Pharaoh went in with the chariots and cavalry into the sea, and the Lord brought on them the water of the sea, but the Israelites walked through dry land in the middle of the sea.

Odes: Chapter 1 Notes

1 Codex Alexandrinus: cyriô (ⲔⲨⲢⲒⲰ). Translation: lord (or master, guardian, ruler, owner)

- Leningrad Codex (in Names): yhvah (יְהוָה).

The Aramaic name Yhů (𐤉𐤄𐤅) was transliterated as Iaô (Ιαω) in some books of the Septuagint, which was later transliterated as Iaw by the Pre-Christian Romans. In later copies of the Septuagint, the name was replaced by the name written in Canaanite Yhůh (𐤉𐤄𐤅𐤄) or Assyrian script Yhůh (יהוה). The name Iaw is found in fragments of the 3rd century AD Papyrus Oxyrhynchus 1007, however, is represented by a double yod ("), meaning it was copied from a later Hebrew or Aramaic text from that era. After the sixth century AD, the occasional copy of the Septuagint is found which uses the name, either written as Iaô (Ιαω) or a Greek approximation of יהוה (ΠΙΠΙ), however, all of these can be traced back to the Hexapla, Quinta, Sextus, and/or Septima, which attempted to retranslate and harmonize the Old Testament in the 3rd through 6th centuries AD.

There are no early surviving copies of the Septuagint's book of Odes that have the name Iaô (Ιαω) in it, and, as the Christians had redacted the name Iaô from their bibles before Odes was created, it is clear it was never in Odes.

The Aramaic sections of Masoretic Daniel that were not translated into Hebrew maintain the term adonai ha'elohim (אֲדֹנָי הָאֱלֹהִים), meaning the 'Lord the gods' where the Septuagint has "Lord the god" (Κύριον τὸν θεὸν), however, the Hebrew sections have Yehvah elohim (יְהוָה אֱלֹהִים)

where the Septuagint has "Lord the god," suggesting the Greek more accurately reflects the Aramaic source texts than the Hebrew translation. According to some records from the time, this was to repair the damage King Manasseh had done 600 years earlier when he removed the name Yahweh from the Israelite Texts, however, no evidence has survived from the era of Manasseh or earlier that proves the name was originally in the text, suggesting it was an attempt by the first Hasmonean High Priest/King Simon the Zealot to create a national Judean religion with a god having a name similar to the Roman god Jove.

2 Codex Alexandrinus: the Masoretic phrase is not found
- Leningrad Codex (in Names): azzi vezimrat yah (עָזִּי וְזִמְרָת יָהּ). Translation: strong (or mighty) and you sang Yah.

The term was either omitted from the Greek translation or missing from the Aramaic texts they translated from. It is unlikely they would have omitted the phrase, as other phrases they did not understand were generally transliterated, suggesting it was either omitted from the Aramaic translation, or added to the Hebrew translation, or its precursor, the Phoenician translation. The shortened form of Yah was used in the Medieval era as a substitute for Yahweh, as the phrase has not survived among the Dead Sea Scrolls, it is possible that it was a late addition to the Torah by the Masoretes, however, that does not seem likely given how much the Dead Sea Scrolls generally match the Leningrad Codex. If the Masoretes were randomly adding phrases to the text they copied, there should be significantly more evidence, and it should conform to Rabbinical Judaism, which is not indicated by this phrase.

The word yah was also used in ancient Canaan as a word meaning "quickly," however if that is what the word meant in this verse, the verse would be very old, as the word does not appear to have been used much after the year 1000 BC to mean "quick." The reference to a female singer suggests that this section of the book of Exodus/Names may have been derived from a song, like the Song of Deborah in the Book of Judges. It is unclear when or why the phrase was dropped from the Aramaic version of Exodus/Names, however, if it was interpreted as a reference to someone singing the Torah, there would have been no reason to leave it in the Aramaic translation.

3 Codex Alexandrinus: cyrios (ⲔⲨⲢⲓⲟⲥ). Translation: lord (or main, chief, dominant, master)

- Leningrad Codex (in Names): Yehvah (יְהוָה)

There are no surviving early fragments of the Septuagint's Exodus that include the name, suggesting the word in the Aramaic version of Exodus/Names was Adonai, which meant "lord" and was also the name of a god in the Canaanite religion, especially in the region around Baalbek, in modern Lebanon. Like the Samaritan Yhů, Adonai was the son of Asherah, suggesting that the Aramaic term in the text that the Greek translation was made from used the name Adonay.

4 Codex Alexandrinus: erythra thalassê (ⲉⲣⲩⲑⲣⲁ ⲑⲁⲗⲁⲥⲥⲏ). Translation: Erythrean Sea (the Red Sea, Gulf of Aden, Persian Gulf, and the Indian Ocean)

- Leningrad Codex (in Names): yam-suf (יַם־סוּף).

Translation: sea of papyrus (or reeds)

The Greek term is not geographically specific, allowing for the Israelites to have passed from Egypt to the wilderness at any point in the Red Sea or even the Gulf of Aden. The Greek name appears to be a translation of the Persian term Erostras, which referred to the entire Persian Gulf, the Red Sea, and the Indian Ocean. The Greeks were likely referring to the Gulf of Suez, however, this was known to the ancient Egyptians as the "Sea of Calm," which is what the Israelites would have called it if that was where they were.

The Hebrew term used in the Masoretic texts, in other books, was yam-suf (יַם־סוּף), meaning "Sea of papyrus." This was not geographically specific either, however, does match the description of the shallow Lake Bardawil which has been a major source for papyrus reeds throughout Egyptian history and is along the described route in Exodus/Names. The Hebrew word suf was virtually identical to the Canaanite word śûp (צוף), also meaning "papyrus" or "reeds," which was in term based on the Egyptian word tjûfî (𓂧𓆑𓏏𓇋), meaning "papyrus plants," or "papyrus marsh." The name was transliterated directly once in the Codex Vaticanus' book of Judges, as thalassês Siph (θαλάσσησ Σιφ), meaning "Sea of Siph," and therefore the Hebrew and Egyptian name is restored in this translation.

5 Codex Alexandrinus: gê (ΓΗ). Translation: Ge (or land, earth, country, soil)

- Leningrad Codex (in Names): aretz (אֶרֶץ). Translation: Eretz (or land, earth, country, soil)

The Earth (Eretz / Ge) is depicted as the same type of primordial deity in the Septuagint as it was in the Greek myths and is called on to witness blessings and curses, implying consciousness. She is described as opening her mouth to swallow things more than once in the Torah, and in other Classical Era Israelite texts, she spoke and had free will, meaning she continued to be seen as a type of goddess by some Israelites until the early Christian era.

Odes: Chapter 2

Song of Moses in Deuteronomy

Watch Shamayim,[1] and I will speak, and let Eretz hear the words out of my mouth. Let my speech be looked for like the rain, and my words come down as dew, as the shower on the plants, and as snow on the grass. For I have called on the name of the Lord, "Assign greatness to our God. As for God, his works are true, and all his ways are judgments, God is faithful, and there is no unrighteousness in him. Just and holy is the Lord. They have sinned, not pleasing him, spotted children, a contrary and perverse generation. Do you, therefore, repay the Lord? Are the people so foolish and unwise? Didn't your father purchase you, and make you, and form you?"

Remember the days of old, consider the ages of ages. Ask your father, and he will tell you, your elders, and they will tell you. When the Highest[2] divided the nations, when he separated the sons of Adam, he divided the borders of the nations according to the number of the messengers of God. The people of Jacob became the portion of the Lord, and Israel was the line of his inheritance. He maintained him in the wilderness, in burning thirst and dry land. He led him about and instructed him, and kept him as the apple of his eye. As an eagle would watch over his brood and yearns over his young, receives them having spread his wings, and takes them up on his back. The Lord alone led them, and there was no alien god with them.

He brought them up on the strength of the land. He fed them with the fruits of the fields. They sucked honey out of the rock, and oil out of the solid rock. Butter of cows, and milk of sheep, with the fat of lambs and rams, of calves and kids, with the fat of kidneys of wheat, and he drank wine, the blood of the grape. So Jacob ate and was filled, and the beloved one kicked, he grew fat, and he became thick and broad. Then he abandoned the god that made him and departed from God his savior. They provoked me to anger with alien gods, with their abominations, they bitterly angered me. They sacrificed to devils, and not to God, but to gods whom they did not know. New and fresh gods came in, who their fathers did not know.

You have forsaken the God that fathered you and forgotten El[3] who feeds you. The Lord saw, and was jealous, and was provoked by the anger of his sons and daughters, and said, "I will turn away my face from them, and will show what will happen to them in the last days, for it is a perverse generation, sons with no faith. They have provoked me to jealousy with that which is not God, they have exasperated me with their idols, and I will provoke them to jealousy with those

224

who are no nation, I will anger them with a nation void of understanding. For a fire has been started from my anger, it will burn to Sheol below, it will devour the land and the fruits of it. It will set on fire the foundations of the mountains. I will gather evils on them and will paralyze them with my weapons. They will be consumed with hunger and the devouring of birds, and there will be irremediable destruction. I will send out against them the teeth of wild beasts, with the rage of serpents creeping on the ground. Outside, the sword will bereave them of children, and terror will issue out of the secret chambers. The young man will perish with the virgin, the suckling with him who has grown old.

I said, "I will scatter them, and I will cause their memorial to cease from among men. Were it not for the anger of the enemy, in case they should live long, in case their enemies should combine against them, in case they should say, 'Our own high arm, and not the Lord, has done all these things.'"

It is a nation that has lost counsel, nor is there under-standing in them. They had no sense to understand. Let them reserve these things against the time to come. How should one pursue a thousand, and two chase tens of thousands, if God had not sold them, and the Lord deliv-ered them up? For their gods are not like our god, but our enemies are void of understanding. For their vine is of the vine of Sodom, and their vine-branch of Gomorrah, their grape is a grape of gall, their cluster is one of bitterness. Their wine is the rage of serpents and the incurable rage of asps.

Look! Are not these things stored up by me, and sealed among my treasures? In the day of vengeance, I will repay them, whenever their foot will be tripped up. The day of their destruction is near to them, and the judgments at hand are close to you. The Lord will judge his people and will be comforted by his servants. For he saw that they were paralyzed, and failed in the hostile invasion, and were become feeble.

The Lord asked, "Where are their gods, in whom they trusted? The fat of whose sacrifices you ate, and you drank the wine of their drink offerings? Let them rise and help you, and be your protectors. Look, know that I am he, and there is no god beside me. I kill, and I will make live. I will kill, and I will heal. None will deliver out of my hands. For I will lift my hand to the sky, and swear by my right hand, and I will say, I live forever. I will sharpen my sword like lightning, and my hand will take hold of judgment. I will render judgment to my enemies and will repay those who hate me. I will make my weapons drunk with blood, and my sword will devour flesh, it will glut itself with the blood of the wounded, and from the captivity of the heads of their enemies that rule over them."

Rejoice, you skies, with him, and let all the messengers of God worship him. Rejoice you Gentiles, with his people, and let all the sons of God strengthen themselves in him. He will avenge the blood of his sons, and he will render vengeance, and repay justice to his enemies, and will reward those who hate him, and the Lord will purge the land of his people.

Odes: Chapter 2 Notes

1 Codex Alexandrinus: ourane (ΟΥΡΑΝΕ). Translation: sky (or Uranus)

• Aleppo Codex (in Words): šmym (שמים). Translation: Shamayim (or skies)

• Leningrad Codex (in Words): shamayim (שָׁמַיִם).
Translation: Shamayim (or skies)

The skies (Shamayim / Uranus) are depicted as the same type of primordial deity in the Septuagint as it was in the Greek myths and called on to witness blessings and curses, implying consciousness. Based on the writings of Jonah and Zephaniah, as well as 4th Kingdoms (Masoretic Kings), Shamayim was a major god in Samaria and Judea before King Josiah's reforms and therefore his name is restored from the Masoretic texts, as he was not known as Uranus. The fact that he is called on by Moses, along with Eretz, means the Song of Moses is much older than the rest of Deuteronomy, and must, if nothing else, date to before King Josiah banned the worship of Shamayim, circa 625 BC.

2 Codex Alexandrinus: ypsistos (ΥﬁΙϹΤΟϹ). Translation: highest
- Aleppo Codex (in Words): ôlyůn (עליון). Translation: highest
- Leningrad Codex (in Words): elyon (עֶלְיוֹן). Translation: highest

El Elyon (Highest God) was the God of Melchizedek, the king of Salem (either Jerusalem or the city of Salem in Samaria) when Abraham passed through Canaan. The term El Elyon is known to have been a major god of the Canaanites, called ål ůålyn (𐤏𐤋𐤉𐤍 𐤀𐤋) in the Sefire Treaty from circa 750 BC. The quotes of Sanchuniathon's writing that have survived to the present, from circa 1200 BC, referred to the god called Elioun as the primordial creator-god of the Canaanites. Most Jewish, Christian, Islamic, and secular historians and archaeologists consider Elyon (highest) to be an epithet of El (God) and not a proper name.

3 Codex Alexandrinus: theou (ΘΕΟΥ). Translation: God
- Aleppo Codex (in Words): ål (אל). Translation: El (or God)
- Leningrad Codex (in Words): el (אֵל). Translation: El (or God)

This verse shows the Greeks did translate the term El as God (Θεου). As El is a proper name, it is restored from the Masoretic texts in this translation.

Odes: Chapter 3

Prayer of Hannah, the Mother of Samuel

My heart is established in the Lord, my horn is exalted in my god. My mouth is enlarged over my enemies. I have rejoiced in your salvation. For there are none as holy as the Lord, and there is none as righteous as our god! There is none holy beside you. Don't brag, and don't speak of high things! Don't let high-sounding words come out of your mouth, for the Lord is a god of knowledge, and god prepares his own designs. The bow of the powerful has become feeble, and the weak have girded themselves with strength.

They who were full of bread are brought low, and the hungry have forgotten the land. The barren has born seven, and she who abounded in children has become feeble. The Lord kills and makes live. He brings down to the grave and brings back up. The Lord makes poor and makes rich. He brings low and lifts up. He lifts up the poor from the earth, and raises the needy from the dunghill, to seat him with the princes of the people, and causes them to inherit the throne of glory, granting the petition to he who prays. He blesses the years of the righteous, for man can't prevail by strength alone."

The Lord will weaken his adversary! The Lord is holy! Don't let the wise man boast of his wisdom, or let the mighty man boast of his strength, or let the rich man boast of his wealth. Instead, let he who boasts, boast of understanding and knowing the Lord, and to executing judgment and justice on the earth. The Lord has gone up to the skies and has thundered. He will judge the extremities of the earth, and he gives strength to our kings and will exalt the horn of his Messiah.[1]

Odes: Chapter 3 Notes

1 Codex Alexandrinus: christou (ⲭⲣⲓⲥⲧⲟⲨ). Translation: Christ

• Dead Sea Scroll 4QSamᵃ (in Samuel): mšyḥ (משׁיח). Translation: Messiah

• Aleppo Codex (in Samuel): mšyh (משיח). Translation: Messiah

• Leningrad Codex (in Samuel): meshicho (מְשִׁיחֹ). Translation: Messiah

All surviving copies of the Septuagint have the word: Christ (Χριστου), which is the Greek translation of the word "Messiah" (מְשִׁיחַ). As the Greek term Christ developed a specific meaning in the Christian era that could not have been intended by the original author, the Jewish term Messiah is used in this translation.

Odes: Chapter 4

Prayer of Habakkuk

Lord, I heard your sound and was carried away.

I considered your works and was amazed.

Between the two living beings, you will be known.

You will be acknowledged when the years draw near.

You will be manifested when the time has come.

When my soul is troubled, you will remember mercy in anger.

The god[1] will come from Teman,[2] and Qetesh[3] out of the mountain covered in the thick forest.[4]

Chant.

His glory obscures Shamayim,[5] and praise of him fills the Earth, and his radiance[6] exists as light,[7] with horns in the hands, and love of its mighty strength.

Before his face will come a report, and it will go out in sandaled feet.

Stopped, and the Earth shook. Looked, and nations melted.

Frightened the fortified hills, and melted the eternal mountains.

Because of troubles, I looked at the quarters of the Kushites.[8]

The tabernacles of the land of Midian will also be dismayed.

Were you angry with the rivers, Lord?

Was your anger against the rivers[9] or against the sea?[10]

You will mount on your horses, and your riding is salvation.

"Certainly you bent your bow at scepters," said the Lord.

Chant.

Rivers burst out of the land observing you, and whirling soldiers scatter water on his course.

Tehom[11] spoke her voice, raising her body on high, "The sun[12] and the moon[13] stop in their path!"[14]

Brightly your fireballs travel at the brilliant flash of your weapons.

You will bring low the land with threatening, and in anger, you will break down the nations.

You went out for the salvation of your people, to save your anointed.

You will bring death on the heads of transgressors, and you have brought shackles on their necks.

Chant.

You cut asunder the heads of princes with amazement, and they will tremble because of it.

They will burst their bridles, they will be like a poor man eating in secret.

You cause your horses to enter the sea, disturbing much water.

I watched, and my belly trembled at the sound of the prayer of my lips, and trembling entered into my bones, and my frame was troubled within me.

I will rest in the day of affliction, from going up to the people of my travels.

For though the fig tree will carry no fruit, and there will be no produce on the vines, the labor of the olive will fail, and the fields will produce no food.

The sheep have failed from the pasture, and there are no oxen in the mangers.

I will celebrate in the Lord, I will celebrate in God,[15] I rejoice.

Lord the god[16] is my strength, and he will perfectly strengthen my feet, when he mounts me on the bamah,[17] that I may conquer by his song.

Odes: Chapter 4 Notes

1 Codex Alexandrinus: o theos (ΟΘΕΟϹ). Translation: the god

- Dead Sea Scroll MurXII (in Habakkuk): ålůh (אלוה). Translation: god
- Aleppo Codex (in Habakkuk): ålůh (אלוה). Translation: god
- Leningrad Codex (in Habakkuk): elovha (אֱלוֹהַ). Translation: god

2 Codex Alexandrinus: Thaeman (ΘΑΙΜΑΝ)
- Dead Sea Scroll MurXII (in Habakkuk): Tymn (תימן)
- Aleppo Codex (in Habakkuk): Tymn (תימן)
- Leningrad Codex (in Habakkuk): Teiman (תֵּימָן)

Teman was the name of a clan of Edomites that lived in the region of Petra, southern Jordan. The archaeological record shows that Yhů was worshiped in both Samaria and Teman around 800 BC, proving the two cultures were closely related.

3 Codex Alexandrinus: agios (ΑΓΙΟϹ). Translation: holy (or saint)
- Dead Sea Scroll MurXII (in Habakkuk): qdůš (קדוש). Translation: Qetesh (or consecration, sanctification)

• Aleppo Codex (in Habakkuk): qdůš (קדוש). Translation:
Qetesh (or consecration, sanctification)

• Leningrad Codex (in Habakkuk): kadosh (קָדוֹשׁ).

Translation: holy (or sacred, saintly)

Qetesh was the title of the goddess Asherah, who was
worshiped in Samaria and Judea at the time of Habakkuk
according to the Septuagint's books of the Kingdoms
(Masoretic Samuel and Kings) and Paralipomena (Masoretic
Divrei-hayyamim), as well as archaeological evidence, such as
the pottery found at Kuntillet Ajrud, in the northeast Sinai,
near the border of modern Egyptian-Israeli border. In various
ancient texts, Qetesh was spelled qdš (קדש), qtš (קטש), qdšt
(קדשת), qůdš (קודש), and qdšů (קדשו).

4 Codex Alexandrinus: ex arous Pharan catasciou daseôs (ΕΞ
ΟΡΟΥϹ ΦΑΡΑΝ ΚΑΤΑϹΚΙΟΥ ΔΑϹΕΩϹ). Translation: out of
Mount Paran covered in thick forest

• Codex Vaticanus (in Habakkuk): ex arous catasciou daseos
(ΕΞ ΟΡΟΥϹ ΚΑΤΑϹΚΙΟΥ ΔΑϹΕΟϹ). Translation: out of the
mountain covered in thick forest

• Dead Sea Scroll MurXII (in Habakkuk): mhr pårn (מהר
פארן). Translation: from Mount Parn

• Aleppo Codex (in Habakkuk): mhr pårn (מהר פארן).

Translation: from Mount Parn.

• Leningrad Codex (in Habakkuk): mehar-paran (מֵהַר־פָּארָן).

Translation: from Mount Paran

The Hebrew word pårn (פארן), does not translate as "out of
the mountain covered in thick forest," which suggests the

Greeks were using a different source text than the Hasmoneans, or the Hasmoneans intentionally added the name Paran. The Wilderness of Paran was mentioned in Cosmic Genesis (Masoretic Bereshít), Numbers, Deuteronomy (Masoretic Words), and 3rd Kingdoms (Masoretic Kings), however, the description in the Septuagint of a "mountain covered in thick forest" does not seem consistent with a desert. The location of Paran is debated, however, the book of Deuteronomy locates it in the Arabah Desert of southern modern Jordan and Israel. In the second century AD, the Christian geographer Claudius Ptolemy located it in the southern Sinai Peninsula, in the region now called the Wadi Feiran, while Islamic scholars have interpreted it as the Hijaz region of western Saudi Arabia, around Mecca.

The difference between the verses in the Septuagint's Habakkuk and Odes indicates that Odes was compiled from Theodotion's retranslation of Habakkuk, from circa 200 AD.

5 Codex Alexandrinus: ecalypsen ouranous (ЄΚΑΛΥϯЄΝ ΟΥΡΑΝΟΥϹ). Translation: concealing (or hiding) Uranus (or sky)

- Dead Sea Scroll MurXII: ksh šmym (כסה שׁמים).
Translation: conceal (or cover) Shamayim (or skies)
- Aleppo Codex (in Habakkuk): ksh šmym (כסה שמים).
Translation: conceal (or cover) Shamayim (or skies)
- Leningrad Codex (in Habakkuk): kissah shamayim (כִּסָּה שָׁמַיִם). Translation: conceal (or cover) Shamayim (or skies)

Shamayim was the Canaanite god of the skies, whose worship was banned by King Josiah of Judah around the time the Neo-Assyrian Empire fell according to 4th Kingdoms (Masoretic Kings), and was also the Lord of the prophet Jonah. Shamayim appears to have been treated as the Canaanite (and Hebrew) name for the Assyrian national god Ashur, in the form of Anshar during the Assyrian rule of Samaria.

6 Codex Alexandrinus: phengos (ⲫⲉⲣⲣⲟⲥ). Translation: light (or radiance, splendor, luster, moonlight, torchlight, glory)
- Dead Sea Scroll MurXII (in Habakkuk): ngh (נגה).
Translation: shine (or radiance, light, shimmering)
- Aleppo Codex (in Habakkuk): ngh (נֹגַהּ). Translation: shine (or radiance, light, shimmering)
- Leningrad Codex (in Habakkuk): nogah (נֹגַהּ). Translation: shine (or radiance, light, shimmering)

7 Codex Alexandrinus: phôs (ⲫⲱⲥ). Translation: light (or man, mortal)
- Dead Sea Scroll MurXII (in Habakkuk): åůr (אור).
Translation: light (or fire)
- Aleppo Codex (in Habakkuk): åůr (אור). Translation: light (or fire)
- Leningrad Codex (in Habakkuk): or (אֹור). Translation: light (or fire)

8 Codex Alexandrinus: Aithiopôn (ΑΙΘΙΟΠΩΝ).

Translation: Ethiopians

• Dead Sea Scroll MurXII (in Habakkuk): kůšn (כושן).

Translation: Kushites (in Aramaic)

• Aleppo Codex (in Habakkuk): kůšn (כושן). Translation:
Kushites (in Aramaic)

• Leningrad Codex (in Habakkuk): chushan (כּוּשָׁ֑ן).

Translation: Kushites (in Aramaic)

"Aethiopia" (Αἰθιοπία) was the Classical Greek translation of
the name of the kingdom of Kush, known as Kesh (𓎡𓈙) in
Old Egyptian, Kash (𓎡𓄿𓈙𓈇) in Late Egyptian, Kaši
(𒆳𒆣) in Akkadian cuneiform, Kas (𓎡𓄿𓈉) in Late
Egyptian, Kasi (𒆳𒅗𒊺) in Neo-Babylonian cuneiform, Kušāya
(𒆳𒆳𒊮𒅀) in Old Persian cuneiform, Chous (Χους) early
Greek, and Kůš (כוש) in Hebrew. As Habakkuk was not
speaking Greek, the older name Kush is imported from the
Masoretic texts.

9 Codex Alexandrinus: potamoes (ΠΟΤΑΜΟΙϹ).

Translation: rivers

• Dead Sea Scroll MurXII: nrhm (נהרים). Translation: rivers

• Aleppo Codex (in Habakkuk): nhrym (נהרים). Translation:
rivers

• Leningrad Codex (in Habakkuk): neharim (נְהָרִים).

Translation: rivers

This reference to the Lord being angry with the rivers and
sea appears to be a reference to the conflict between Lord

Hadad and Lord Yam (sea) in the Baal Cycle. Yam was also known as Judge Nahor (river).

10 Codex Alexandrinus: thalassê (ѲⲀⲗⲗⲀϹϹн). Translation: sea

- Dead Sea Scroll MurXII (in Habakkuk): ym (ים).
Translation: sea (or Yam)
- Aleppo Codex (in Habakkuk): ym (ים). Translation: sea (or Yam)
- Leningrad Codex (in Habakkuk): yam (יָם). Translation: sea (or Yam)

This reference to the Lord being angry with the rivers and sea appears to be a reference to the conflict between Lord Hadad and Lord Yam (sea) in the Baal Cycle. Yam was also known as Judge Nahor (river).

11 Codex Alexandrinus: abyssos (ⲀⲃⲨϹϹОⲤ). Translation: abyss

- Dead Sea Scroll MurXII (in Habakkuk): thŭm (תהום).
Translation: primordial waters
- Aleppo Codex (in Habakkuk): thŭm (תהום). Translation: primordial waters
- Leningrad Codex (in Habakkuk): tehom (תְהוֹם).
Translation: primordial waters

The abyss is a common element in most ancient Middle Eastern religions. In Egyptian beliefs, the abyss was called Nun (𓏌𓏲𓈖), meaning "sky waters," and like many of the other religions, this sea was seen as being a cosmic sea, both below the Earth, and above the Sky, and reaching off to infinity. The cosmic sea was an early attempt to envision what is now called outer space, assumed to be composed of freshwater.

The Sumerian name for the primordial waters was [deity]Nammu (✳▣), however, they also referred to it as abzu (▣▦), meaning "deep water," and zuab (▦▣), meaning 'water deep.' The Greek name abyssou may have been derived from the Sumerian term abzu, however, does not appear to have been imported to Greek thought until the early Iron Age, as the word is not found in the Linear-B script of the Bronze Age. The Akkadians called the Abyss tâmtu (▦▣▣), which meant "lakes," however, the god that lived in it was replaced with Ia (▣▦), whose name is believed to be derived from the Sumerian words "praise" (▣) and "water" (▦). The transliteration of the word as Ia is modern, and if transliterated in Akkadian, the name would have been Ṣēriš Muú, meaning "praise water," or "sacred water."

Ia replaced the earlier Sumerian god [an]Enki (✳▦◈), whose name translates as [deity]Lord Earth. During the Old Babylonian era, Ia was replaced by [an]Nabu (✳▦), the sun-calf [an]Marduk's son, and the personification of the planet Mercury in Babylonian cosmology. In Babylonian cosmology, the deity of the Abyss tâmtu was [an]Timimat (✳◁◈), generally transliterated into English a Tiamat.

Both tâmtu and Tiamat are recorded in Ugaritic as thm (▬▣) and Thmt (▬▣▬), indicating they were separate concepts in bronze age Canaan. In the book of Habakkuk, written around 612 BC, the goddess was referred to as Tehom (תְּהוֹם), presumably in Judahite, the precursor to Classical Hebrew which was written in the Canaanite script. By the era of Habakkuk, the Israelites had been living in Canaan for centuries, and the word yam (יָם) had replaced təhôm as the word meaning seas, meaning that he had to be referring to the goddess.

12 Codex Alexandrinus: Êlios (Ηλιος). Translation: Helios (or sun)
- Dead Sea Scroll MurXII (in Habakkuk): šmš (שׁמשׁ).
Translation: Shemesh (or sun)
- Aleppo Codex (in Habakkuk): šmš (שֶׁמֶשׁ). Translation:
Shemesh (or sun)
- Leningrad Codex (in Habakkuk): šemeš (שֶׁמֶשׁ).
Translation: Shemesh (or sun)

13 Codex Alexandrinus: Selênê (СελнΝн). Translation:
Selene (or moon)
- Dead Sea Scroll MurXII (in Habakkuk): -ḥ (ח-). Only the final letter of the name survives, however, it does support the name being in the text. Dead Sea Scroll MurXII dates to the early Roman Period (6 to 135 AD).
- Aleppo Codex (in Habakkuk): yrḥ (ירח). Translation:
Yarikh (or moon)
- Leningrad Codex (in Habakkuk): yareach (יָרֵחַ).
Translation: Yarikh (or moon)

14 Codex Alexandrinus: ho hêlios cae hê selênê estê en tê taxi autês (O HⲀIOC KⲀI H CEⲀHNH ECTH EN TH TⲀⲎEI ⲀYTHC). Translation: the sun (or Helios) and the moon (or Selene) stop in position (or ordering, rank, post, place, arrangement) his

• Codex Vaticanus (in Habakkuk): epêrthê ho hêlios, cae hê selênê estê en tê taxi autês (EⲠHPⲐH O HⲀIOC KⲀI H CEⲀHNHECTHENTHTⲀⲎEIⲀYTHC). Translation: Raise the sun (or Helios), and the moon (or Selene) stop in position (or ordering, rank, post, place, arrangement) his

• Aleppo Codex Habakkuk reads: šmš yrh ômd zblh (שמש ירח עמד זבלה). Translation: Shemesh (or sun) Yarikh (or moon) stand (in Hebrew, or 'sink' in Aramaic) to home (or residence)

• Leningrad Codex (in Habakkuk): shemesh yareach amad zevulah (שֶׁמֶשׁ יָרֵחַ עָמַד זְבֻלָה). Translation: Shemesh (or sun) Yarikh (or moon) stand (in Hebrew, or 'sink' in Aramaic) to home (or residence)

The versions of this verse in the Septuagint's Habakkuk and Odes are different, with the version in Odes supporting the Odes being based on Theodotion's translation of circa 200 AD.

15 Codex Alexandrinus: theô (ⲐEW). Translation: god

• Dead Sea Scroll MurXII (in Habakkuk): the word is damaged, however, å-hy (א-הי) survives, and the entire word ålhy (אלהי) survives earlier in the text. Translation: god (in Aramaic), divine (in Hebrew)

• Aleppo Codex (in Habakkuk): ålhy (‏אלהי‎). Translation: god (in Aramaic), divine (in Hebrew)

• Leningrad Codex (in Habakkuk): alohei (‏אֱלֹהֵי‎).

Translation: god (in Aramaic), divine (in Hebrew)

16 Codex Alexandrinus: Cyrios ho theos (ΚΥΡΙΟϹΟΘΕΟϹ). Translation: Lord the god

• Dead Sea Scroll MurXII (in Habakkuk): the term is damaged, however, yhůh å- (-‏א יהוה‎) survives, indicating the term was present.

• Aleppo Codex (in Habakkuk): yhůh ådny (‏יהוה אדני‎).

Translation: Yhůh my lord

• Leningrad Codex (in Habakkuk): yehvih adonai (‏יְהוִה‎

‏אֲדֹנָי‎). Translation: Yehvih lord

The Aramaic sections of Masoretic Daniel that were not translated into Hebrew maintain the term adonai ha'elohim (‏אֲדֹנָי הָאֱלֹהִים‎), meaning the 'Lord the gods' where the Septuagint has "Lord the god" (Κύριον τὸν θεὸν), however, the Hebrew sections have Yehvah elohim (‏יְהוָה אֱלֹהִים‎) where the Septuagint has "Lord the god," suggesting the Greek more accurately reflects the Aramaic source texts than the Hebrew translation. According to some records from the time, this was to repair the damage King Manasseh had done 600 years earlier when he removed the name Yahweh from the Israelite Texts, however, no evidence has survived from the era of Manasseh or earlier that proves the name was originally in the text. In this case, the term "Yehvih lord" (‏יְהוָה אֲדֹנָי‎) is used in the Masoretic texts where the Greek translation has "Lord the god" (Κύριοσ ὁ θεὸσ), indicating that the Aramaic text of Habakkuk was not translated directly in Hebrew.

17 Codex Alexandrinus: hypsêla (ⲨⳎⲎⲗⲗ). Translation: high up
- Aleppo Codex (in Habakkuk): bmůty (בְמֹתִי). Translation: bamahs
- Leningrad Codex (in Habakkuk): bamovtai (בָּמוֹתֵי).

Translation: bamahs

Bamahs were stone platforms built at the tops of hills, where sacrifices were made to gods in ancient Canaan and Assyria. These Bamahs generally included an altar for barbecuing the sacrifices, a stele, a seat for the god (which the priest would sit on), a tree representing Asherah (Ashteroth), and a cistern for water. These Bamahs were also generally accompanied by a banquet hall, and a "low stone" used for slaughtering and butchering the animal.

Bamah's were banned during the reign of Kings Hezekiah, circa 716 to 697 BC, relegalized by his heir King Manasseh, and then banned and destroyed by King Josiah, circa 640 to 609 BC, meaning that Habakkuk could not have been in Judah at the time. Bamahs were also used in Amman, Moab, and Babylonian-occupied Samaria and Syria at the time, meaning Habakkuk must have been in one of these lands.

Odes: Chapter 5

Prayer of Isaiah

From night until dawn, my spirit seeks you, God, for your commandments are a light on the earth. Learn righteousness, you that live on the earth. For the ungodly one is put down, and no one who will not learn righteousness on the earth will be able to do the truth. Let the ungodly be taken away, so he does not see the glory of the Lord.

Lord, your arm is exalted, yet they did not know it, When they learn it, they will be ashamed, jealousy will seize on an untaught nation, and now fire will consume the enemies. Lord God, give us peace, for you have given us all things.

Lord God, take possession of us, Lord, we know not any other beside you, and we name your name, but the dead will not see life, neither will physicians by any means raise them up, therefore, you have brought anger on them, and slain them, and have taken away every male of them.

Bring more evils on them, Lord, bring more evils on the glorious ones of the earth. Lord, in affliction I remembered you, your punishment was for us with small affliction.

Like a pregnant woman draws near her delivery date and cries out in her pain, so have we been to your beloved. We are conceived, Lord, because of your fear, and have been in pain, and have brought out the breath of your salvation, which we have worked on the earth, we will not fall, but all that live on the land will fall.

The dead will rise, and those who are in the tombs will be raised, and those who are in the earth will rejoice. For the dew from you is healing to them, but the land of the ungodly will perish. Go, my people, enter into your closets, shut your door, and hide for a little while, until the anger of the Lord has passed away.

Odes: Chapter 6

Prayer of Jonah

I cried in my affliction to the Lord my god,[1] and he listened to me, even to my cry out of the belly of Sheol.[2] You heard my voice. You threw me into the depths of the heart of the sea, and the waters surrounded me, and all your billows and your waves have passed on me.

I said, "I am thrown out of your presence. Will I ever see your holy temple again? Water was poured around me to the mind, the lowest depths surrounded me, and my head went down to the clefts of the mountains. I went down into the earth, whose bars are the ever-lasting barriers, yet, Lord God, let my ruined life be restored. When my soul was failing me, I remembered the Lord, and may my prayer come to you into your holy temple. They who observe vain and false things have forgotten their own mercy, but I will sacrifice to you with the voice of praise and thanksgiving! All that I have vowed I will pay to you, as a thanks-offering to the Lord."

Odes: Chapter 6 Notes

1 Codex Alexandrinus: cyrion ton theon mou (ΚΥΡΙΟΝ ΤΟΝΘΕΟΝΜΟΥ). Translation: Lord my god

• Aleppo Codex (in Jonah): ål yhůh (אל יהוה). Translation: god Yhůh

- Leningrad Codex (in Jonah): el-yehvah (אֶל־יְהוָה).

Translation: to (or towards, into, at, by) Yehvah

2 Codex Alexandrinus: adou (ⲀⲓⲆⲞⲨ). Translation: Hades
- Aleppo Codex (in Jonah): šåůl (שְׁאוֹל). Translation: underworld
- Leningrad Codex (in Jonah): she'ol (שְׁאוֹל). Translation: underworld

Hades is the Greek name for a section of the underworld ruled by the god Hades. The definition of Sheol is less clear, as the Hebrews used the term more loosely. In this sentence, the author likely meant "abyss" or depths.

Odes: Chapter 7

Prayer of Azariah

Blessed are you, Lord, God of our fathers, and worthy of praise. Your name is to be praised forever. You are just in all that you have done to us, and all your works are true and your ways right, and all your judgments are just.

You have executed just judgments in all that you have brought on us, and on Jerusalem, the holy city of our fathers, for in truth and justice you have brought all this on us because of our sins. We have sinfully and lawlessly departed from you, and have sinned in all things and have not obeyed your commandments, we have not observed them or done them, as you have commanded us so it might go well with us.

So all that you have brought on us, and all that you have done to us, you have done in true judgment. You have given us into the hands of lawless enemies, most hateful rebels, and to an unjust king, the most wicked in all the world. Now we cannot open our mouths, shame and disgrace have happened to your servants and worshipers. For your name's sake do not give us up completely, and do not break your covenant, and do not withdraw your mercy from us, for the sake of Abraham your beloved and for the sake of Isaac your servant and Israel your holy one, to whom you promised to make their descendants as many as the stars of the sky and as the sand on the shore of the sea.

We, Lord, have become fewer than any nation, and are brought low this day in all the world because of our sins. At this time there is no prince, prophet, or leader, no burnt offering, sacrifice, oblation, or incense, no place to make an offering before you or to find mercy. Yet with a contrite heart and a humiliated spirit may we be accepted, as though it were with burnt offerings of rams and bulls, and with tens of thousands of fat lambs, such may our sacrifice be in your sight this day, and may we wholly follow you, for there will be no shame for those who trust in you.

Now with all our heart, we follow you, we fear you and seek your face. Do not put us to shame, but deal with us in your patience and your abundant mercy. Deliver us by your marvelous works, and give glory to your name, Lord! Let all who harm your servants be put to shame, and let them be disgraced and deprived of all power and dominion, and let their strength be broken.

Let them know that you are the Lord, the only God, glorious over the whole world.

Odes: Chapter 8

Hymn to Our Father

Blessed are you Lord, the god of our fathers, and to be praised and exalted above all forever.

Blessed is your glorious and holy name, and to be praised and exalted above all forever.

Blessed are you in the temple[1] of your sacred glory, and to be praised and glorified above all forever.

Blessed are you who see the depths, and ride on the sphinxes,[2] and to be praised and exalted above all forever.

Blessed are you on the glorious throne of your kingdom, and to be praised and glorified above all forever.

Blessed are you in the firmament of the sky,[3] and above all to be praised and glorified forever.

Bless the Lord, works of the Lord, and praise and exalt him above all forever.

Bless the Lord, messengers of the Lord, and praise and exalt him above all forever.

Bless the Lord, Shamayim,[4] and praise and exalt him above all forever.

Bless the Lord, all waters above the sky,[5] and praise and exalt him above all forever.

Bless the Lord, all the forces,[6] and praise and exalt him above all forever.

Bless the Lord, Shemesh and Yarikh,[7] and praise and exalt him above all forever.

Bless the Lord, stars of the skies,[8] and praise and exalt him above all forever.

Bless the Lord, all thunderstorms and rain, and praise and exalt him above all forever.

Bless the Lord, all winds, and praise and exalt him above all forever.

Bless the Lord, fire and glow, and praise and exalt him above all forever.

Bless the Lord, cold and heat, and praise and exalt him above all forever.

Bless the Lord, dew and falling snow, and praise and exalt him above all forever.

Bless the Lord, frost and ice, and praise and exalt him above all forever.

Bless the Lord, hoar-frost and slush, and praise and exalt him above all forever.

Bless the Lord, nights and days, and praise and exalt him above all forever.

Bless the Lord, light and darkness, and praise and exalt him above all forever.

Bless the Lord, lightning and clouds, and praise and exalt him above all forever.

Bless the Lord, Eretz,[9] and praise and exalt him above all forever.

Bless the Lord, mountains and hills, and praise and exalt him above all forever.

Bless the Lord, everything growing out of the land, and praise and exalt him above all forever.

Bless the Lord, springs,[10] and praise and exalt him above all forever.

Bless the Lord, seas and rivers, and praise and exalt him above all forever.

Bless the Lord, Cetus and those moving in the rain-water,[11] and praise and exalt him above all forever.

Bless the Lord, all who fly in the sky, and praise and exalt him above all forever.

Bless the Lord, humans,[12] and praise and exalt him above all forever.

Bless the Lord, Israel, and praise and exalt him above all forever.

Bless the Lord, priests of the Lord, and praise and exalt him above all forever.

Bless the Lord, slaves of the Lord, and praise and exalt him above all forever.

Bless the Lord, spirits and minds of the righteous, and praise and exalt him above all forever.

Bless the Lord, pious and humble of heart, and praise and exalt him above all forever.

Bless the Lord, Hananiah, Azariah, and Mishael, and praise and exalt him above all forever.

Odes: Chapter 8 Notes

1 Codex Alexandrinus: naô (ΝΑѠ). Translation: temples (or shrines)

The prayer of the three youths is not in the Masoretic version of Daniel. This chapter is set in the 18th year of King Nebuchadnezzar II, which was 587 BC, during the siege of Jerusalem (589-586 BC). Regardless of the reason given in the text, Nebuchadnezzar's actions to remove the three Judahites from office during the siege is consistent with the political setting of the chapter. At the time the prayer was supposedly spoken, King Solomon's Temple was still standing, and it seems likely that the prayer section would have been removed from the Hebrew translations because the temple was torn down the following year, and this prayer, assuming it happened as described, may have been one of the reasons for its destruction.

2 Codex Alexandrinus: cheroubin (ⲭⲉⲣⲟⲩⲃⲓⲛ). Translation: cherubs (or griffins, sphinxes)

While the Masoretic version of Daniel does not include the prayer, the terms used in the Greek translations are transliterations of Aramaic and Hebrew spellings of the word krûbyn (ץ^ץ٦ץ) and keruvim (כְּרוּבִים). Theodition's transliteration of cheroubin (χερουβιν), which ended up in the Codex Vaticanus, and most other copies of the Orthodox Christian Septuagint, is a transliteration from the Aramaic and not Hebrew version of the word, supporting it having been in an Aramaic version of the prayer in Theodotion's time.

The word 'cherub" (בהגב / כרוב / ץעעץ / ༩٩४) was the West Semitic term for the mythical creature generally called a "griffin" today. Based on the archaeological record of Canaan, it appears that the concept of the cherub was based on the Egyptian sphinx, as the earliest cherub statues found in Canaan were Egyptian statues of sphinxes. Archaeologists are not sure if the griffins of Anatolia were based on the Canaanite cherub, or the Egyptian sphinxes directly, however, all three mythical beings are closely related in the archaeological record.

The term cherub was for some reason reinterpreted as "baby angels" by Christians, although in the Books of the Kingdoms, God was described as riding on cherubs, and it is not clear why any god would ride around on "baby angels," therefore the alternate translation of "sphinxes" is used in this translation, as it is in later books of the Septuagint, as the concept of a Neo-Assyrian karâbu (ᵉᴴᴴᴱᴴᵡ⊢) would have been anachronistic before the early iron age. In this verse, girtablilû may be a more accurate translation, however, was probably no longer understood in the era when the Israelites left Egypt, as even the Babylonians were no longer commonly using the term.

3 Codex Alexandrinus: stereômati tou ouranou (CTEPEШMATI TOY OYPANOY). Translation: framework the skies, foundation the skies, vaulted sky
The prayer of the three youths is not in the Masoretic version of Daniel.

4 Codex Alexandrinus: ouranoe (OYPANOI). Translation: skies
The prayer of the three youths is not in the Masoretic version of Daniel. The term ouranoe (Οὐρανοί) was the Greek translation of the Aramaic word šmyn (ʾ^ʾʑ), meaning "skies." The term was both the word for "skies" and the name of the god of the skies, the Canaanite version of the Greek Uranus, Akkadian An, and Egyptian Nut. In the late Bronze Age Ugaritic language, the word for skies was spelled šmm (⟨ᵖᵀᵀᵀ⟩), while the name of the god was Šmyn (⟨ᵖᵀᵀᵐ⟩). The two words survived into Aramaic as šmyå (N^ʾʑ), meaning "sky," and Šmyn (ʾ^ʾʑ), the name of the god of the skies, which is the term translated in this verse.

5 Codex Alexandrinus: ydata panta ta epanô tou ouranou (ΥΔΑΤΑ ΠΑΝΤΑ ΤΑ ΕΠΑΝΩ ΤΟΥ ΟΥΡΑΝΟΥ). Translation: fresh-water all above the sky

The prayer of the three youths is not in the Masoretic version of Daniel. In the flat-earth theory of the Bronze Age and early Iron Age, above the Vaulted Sky, was an ocean of fresh water, which was where the rain fell from. In the Ugaritic Texts, the rain was described as falling from the stars, which were viewed as being holes in the vaulted sky.

6 Codex Alexandrinus: dynamis (ΔΥΝΑΜΕΙϹ). Translation: forces

The prayer of the three youths is not in the Masoretic version of Daniel.

7 Codex Alexandrinus: êlios cae selênê (ΗΛΙΟϹ ΚΑΙ ϹΕΛΗΝΗ). Translation: sun and moon, Helois (Greek sun god) and Selene (Greek moon goddess)

The prayer of the three youths is not in the Masoretic version of Daniel. According to 4th Kingdoms, the Judahites worshiped the sun and the moon as gods at the time, therefore the Canaanite (Hebrew) names of the gods are restored in this translation, as they are clearly who are being referenced.

8 Codex Alexandrinus: astra tou ouranou (ΑϹΤΡΑΤΟΥ ΟΥΡΑΝΟΥ). Translation: stars of the sky

The prayer of the three youths is not in the Masoretic version of Daniel.

9 Codex Alexandrinus: Gê (ⲅⲏ). Translation: Ge (or earth, land)

The prayer of the three youths is not in the Masoretic version of Daniel. The Canaanite and Israelite version of the earth goddess was Eretz, which was recorded in many ancient Canaanite texts, including the Masoretic texts, and therefore that name is restored in this text.

10 Codex Alexandrinus: pêgae (ⲡⲏⲅⲁⲓ). Translation: springs

The prayer of the three youths is not in the Masoretic version of Daniel.

11 Codex Alexandrinus: cêtê cae panta ta cinoumena en toes hydasin (ⲕⲏⲧⲏ ⲕⲁⲓ ⲡⲁⲛⲧⲁ ⲧⲁ ⲕⲓⲛⲟⲩⲙⲉⲛⲁ ⲉⲛ ⲧⲟⲓⲥ ⲩⲇⲁⲥⲓⲛ). Translation: Cetus (or whale, dolphin, sea monster) and everything moving in the freshwater (or rainwater, time, sky-water)

The prayer of the three youths is not in the Masoretic version of Daniel. The Greek translation is strange, as whales and other sea creatures do not swim around in rain or freshwater, they swim in the sea. Both the Greek and Canaanite languages used different terms for freshwater and seawater. The Greeks also didn't translate the term as spring or river, suggesting the Aramaic term was myå (𐡀𐡉𐡌), not ymå (𐡌𐡉𐡀), meaning that this was the water in the sky, not the water in the sea. Therefore, the word translated as cêtê (κήτη) would have to be a word representing Cetus, and the other things moving in the sky would have been the other constellations. Cetus was among the 'water constellations' Aquarius, Pisces, and Eridanus, which dominated the sky above Canaan during the winter months of the late Bronze Age and early Iron Age, when most of the water fell from the stars in the Canaanite religion. As the constellations moved in both the fresh water above the sky, and time, the word hydasin (ὕδασιν) translates as both "rainwater" and "time." Assuming the prayer was translated from an Aramaic text, the likely name of the constellation was Lůytn (𐤋𐤅𐤉𐤕𐤍), with was translated as Cetus (κήτη) in other books of the Septuagint. The Aramaic name of Lůytn (𐤋𐤅𐤉𐤕𐤍), was descended from the Ugaritic Ltn (𐎍𐎚𐎐), the sea monster of Late Bronze Age Canaan. The name appears in the Masoretic texts as Lůůyytn (לוייתן), which is generally transliterated as Leviathan in English.

12 Codex Vaticanus: hoe huioe tôn anthrôpôn (ΟΙΥΙΟΙΤѠΝ ΑΝΘΡѠΠѠΝ). Translation: the sons of the men, humans

The prayer of the three youths is not in the Masoretic version of Daniel.

Odes: Chapter 9

Prayer of Zachariah

Praised be the Lord, God in Israel, for he has visited and redeemed his people, and has raised a horn of salvation for us in the house of his servant David, as he said by the mouth of his holy prophets from of old so that we should be saved from our enemies, and from the hand of all who hate us. To perform the mercy promised to our fathers, and to remember his holy covenant, the oath which he swore to our father Abraham, to grant us that we, being delivered from the hand of our enemies, might serve him without fear, in holiness and lawfulness before him, all the days of our life.

You, child, will be called the prophet of the Highest, as you will go before the Lord to prepare his ways, to give knowledge of salvation to his people in the forgiveness of their sins, through the tender mercy of our God, when the day will dawn on us from on high to give light to those who sit in darkness and in the shadow of death, to guide our feet into the way of peace.

Odes: Chapter 10

Song of Isaiah

Now I will sing to my beloved, a song of my beloved about my vineyard.

My beloved had a vineyard on a high hill in a fertile place, where I planted a hedge around it, and dug a trench. I planted a choice vine and built a tower in it. I dug a place for the wine-vat in it, and I waited for it to grow grapes, but it brought out thorns.

Now, you residents in Jerusalem, and every man of Judah, judge between me and my vineyard. What will I do anymore to my vineyard, that I have not done for it? Whereas I expected it to grow grapes, but it has grown thorns.

Now I will tell you what I will do to my vineyard! I will take away its hedge, and it will be ruined, and I will pull down its walls, and it will be left to be trodden down. I will ignore my vineyard, and it will not be pruned or dug, and thorns will grow up on it like on barren land, for I will command the clouds to rain no rain on it.

The vineyard of Lord Sabaoth[1] is the house of Israel, and the men of Judah are his beloved plant. I expected it to bring our judgment, and it brought out iniquity. Not righteousness but crying. Woe to those who combine houses and add fields together so they may take away something from their neighbors. Will you live alone on the land? These things have reached the ears of Lord Sabaoth.

Odes: Chapter 10 Notes

1 Codex Alexandrinus: Cyrios Sabaôth (ΚΥΡΙΟϹϹΑΒΑѠΘ). Translation: Lord Sabaoth

- Great Isaiah Scroll: yhůh ṣbåůt (יהוה צבאות). Translation: Yhůh of armies

- Aleppo Codex (in Isaiah): yhůh ṣbåůt (יהוה צבאות). Translation: Yhůh of armies

- Leningrad Codex (in Isaiah): yehvah tzeva'ot (יְהוָה צְבָאוֹת). Translation: Yahweh of armies

The fact that the term cyrios ho pantocratôr (κύριος ὁ παντοκράτωρ) is missing in the book of Isaiah, implies the Greek translation was likely made from a Hebrew translation that the Maccabees had already partially redacted, which would date the translation to between 165 and 140 BC. In most of the books of prophecy, the Septuagint has the term Lord Almighty (κύριος ὁ παντοκράτωρ) where the Masoretic texts have Yahweh of armies (יְהוָה צְבָאוֹת). In the Book of Job, which was not redacted by the Hasmoneans, the term Almighty (παντοκράτωρ) was the Greek translation of Shaddai (שַׁדַּי), meaning "demons," which implies that the original term in Isaiah may have also been Shaddai, however, no older copies are known to exist that could confirm this.

After the Septuagint's copy of Isaiah, which dates to shortly before 140 BC, the oldest known copies are found among the Dead Sea Scrolls and date to the Hasmonean and Herodian eras, between 140 BC and 6 AD.

Odes: Chapter 11

Prayer of Hezekiah

I said at the end of my days, "I will go to the gates of Sheol, and I will part with the remainder of my years."

I said, "I will never again see the salvation of God in the land of the living. I will never again see the salvation of Israel on the Earth. I will never again see man. My life has failed from among my families. I have parted with the remainder of my life, and it has gone out and departed from me, as one that has pitched a tent takes it down again, my breath was with me as a weaver's web when she that weaves draws near to cut off the thread."

On that day I was given up as to a lion until the morning, so has he broken all my bones, for I was so given up from the day until the night.

Like a swallow, so will I cry, and like a dove, so do I mourn, for my eyes have failed to see the heights of the sky of the Lord, who has delivered me, and removed the sorrow of my mind.

Lord, it was told to you about this, and you have revived my breath, and I am comforted and live.

You have chosen my soul, that it should not perish, and you have thrown all sins behind me.

For they that are in the grave will not praise you, neither will the dead bless you, neither will they that are in Sheol hope for your mercy.

The living will bless you, as I also do, for from this day will I father children, who will declare your righteousness, God of my salvation, and I will not cease blessing you with the psaltery all the days of my life before the house of God.

Odes: Chapter 12

Prayer of Manasseh

Lord Almighty[1] the god of our forefathers Abraham, Isaac, and Jacob and of their righteous descendants, he who has made the sky and the earth with all their adornment. He who has bound the sea with the word of your commandment. He who has closed the abyss[2] and sealed it with your fearful and glorious name. He whom all things revere and tremble before the face of your power because the magnificence of your glory is unendurable and irresistible the anger of your threatening against sinners. The mercy of your promise is both immeasurable and inscrutable, for you are the Highest,[3] compassionate, patient, and most merciful, forgiving of the evils of men. You, Lord, according to the abundance of your goodness, have proclaimed repentance and forgiveness to those that have sinned against you, and in the multitude of your kindnesses, you have decreed for sinners repentance to salvation.

Certainly, you, Lord the god of justice, have not appointed repentance for the just, for Abraham, Isaac, and Jacob who have not sinned against you, but you have appointed repentance for me a sinner. I have sinned more than the number of the sand of the sea. My transgressions are multiplied, Lord, they are multiplied, and I am not worthy to look at or see the height of the sky, for the multitude of my iniquities, being bowed down by many iron bonds, so that I can't uplift my head, and there is no release for me, because I have provoked your anger, and have done evil before you, not doing your will, nor keeping your commandments, but setting up abominations and multiplying offence.

Now, I bend the knee of my heart, begging your goodness. I have sinned, Lord, I have sinned, and I acknowledge my transgressions, but I pray and beg you, release me, Lord, release me, and destroy me not with my transgressions. Don't keep me in evil anger forever, nor condemn me to the lowest parts of the Earth, because you are God, the god of the repenting. You will show all your benevolence in saving me. Although I am unworthy, you will save me in your great mercy. I will praise you continually all the days of my life. All the forces of the skies sing to you, and yours is the glory forever and ever, Amen.[4]

Odes: Chapter 12 Notes

1 Codex Alexandrinus: cyrie pantocratôr (ⲕ Ⲩ ⲣ ⲓ ⲉ ⲡ ⲁ ⲛ ⲧ ⲟ ⲕ ⲣ ⲁ ⲧ ⲱ ⲣ). Translation lord almighty (or all-powerful).

The books of Septuagint's Book of 4th Kingdoms (Masoretic Kings), both clearly report that Manasseh re-instituted Baalism in Judea when he became king, suggesting that this reference was to Ba'al. He is also known from Assyrian records and is, therefore, one of the few early kings of Judah that is attested by independent records. As Manasseh was considered one of the most "evil" kings by the Levitical authors of 4th Kingdoms (Masoretic Kings), because he restored the land to Baalism, and restored the statue of Baal in the Temple of Solomon, it is likely that this prayer is to Ba'al, whose name means "lord" in Canaanite bôl (𐤋𐤏𐤁), Aramaic bôlå (𐡁𐡋𐡏), and Hebrew ba'al (בַּעַל).

2 Codex Alexandrinus: abysson (ΑΒΥϹϹΟΝ). Translation: abyss (or underworld, deep sea)

The abyss is a common element in most ancient Middle Eastern religions. In Egyptian beliefs, the abyss was called Nun (𓈖𓈖𓈖𓈗), meaning "sky waters," and like many of the other religions, this sea was seen as being a cosmic sea, both below the Earth, and above the Sky, and reaching off to infinity. The cosmic sea was an early attempt to envision what is now called outer space, assumed to be composed of freshwater.

The Sumerian name for the primordial waters was [deity]Nammu (𒀭𒇉), however, they also referred to it as abzu (𒍪𒀊), meaning "deep water," and zuab (𒀊𒍪), meaning "water deep." The Greek name abyssou may have been derived from the Sumerian term abzu, however, does not appear to have been imported to Greek thought until the early Iron Age, as the word is not found in the Linear-B script of the Bronze Age. The Akkadians called the Abyss tâmtu (𒋾𒄠𒌓), which meant "lakes," however, the god that lived in it was replaced with Ia (𒂍𒀀), whose name is believed to be derived from the Sumerian words "praise" (𒂍) and "water" (𒀀). The transliteration of the word as Ia is modern, and if transliterated in Akkadian, the name would have been Ṣēriš Muú, meaning "praise water."

Ia replaced the earlier Sumerian god [an]Enki (𒀭𒂗𒆠), whose name translates as [deity]Lord Earth. During the Old Babylonian era, Ia was replaced by [an]Nabu (𒀭𒈾), the [deity]Sun-calf [an]Marduk's son, and the personification of the planet Mercury in Babylonian cosmology. In Babylonian cosmology, the deity of the Abyss tâmtu was [an]Timimat (𒀭𒋾𒀀𒆳), generally transliterated into English a Tiamat.

Both tâmtu and Tiamat are recorded in Ugaritic as thm (𐎚𐎅𐎎) and Thmt (𐎚𐎅𐎎𐎚), indicating they were separate concepts in bronze age Canaan. In the book of Habakkuk, written around 612 BC, the goddess was referred to as Tehom (תְּהוֹם), presumably in Judahite, the precursor to Classical Hebrew which was written in the Canaanite script.

3 Codex Alexandrinus: ypsistos (Ⲩⲯⲓⲥⲧⲟⲥ). Translation: highest

The Highest is a reference to God, or a god, found in many ancient religions in the region. According to the Torah, the ancient people of Jerusalem worshiped El Elyon, which translates as "Highest God" when Abraham passed through the regions. The term Highest repeats through other early Canaanite, Samaritan, Judahite, and Greek texts.

4 Codex Alexandrinus: amên (Ⲁⲙⲏⲛ)

272

Odes: Chapter 13

Prayer of Simeon

Lord, let your servant leave in peace, according to your word, as my eyes have seen your salvation, which you have prepared in the presence of all peoples. A light of revelation to the Gentiles, and for glory to your people Israel.

Odes: Chapter 14

Morning Hymn

Honor the highest god, and on earth peace and good-will to man.

We praise you, we bless you, we worship you, we glorify you, and we thank you, for your great glory.

Lord King, celestial, almighty father god.

Unique child of the Lord, Jesus Christ, Lord the god.

The lamb of God, the Son of the Father, who takes away the sin of the world, have mercy on us, who takes away the sin of the world, accept our prayers.

You who sit at the right of the Father, have mercy on us.

For you are the only Holy One, you are the only Lord, Jesus Christ, to the glory of God the Father.

Amen.

Every evening I will bless you, and I will praise your name forever, and to the centuries of centuries.

Grant, Lord, that in this night we may be kept without sin.

Blessed are you, Lord, the god of our Fathers, and praised and glorified is your name to the ages.

Amen.

Blessed are you, Lord, teach me your rules of life.

Blessed are you, Lord, teach me your rules of life.

Blessed are you, Lord, teach me your rules of life.

Lord, you have become for us a refuge from generation to generation.

I have said, 'Lord, have mercy on me, heal my soul for I have sinned against you.'

Lord, I have fled to you. Teach me to do your will for you are my God.

With you is the fountain of life, and in your light, we will see light.

Extend your mercy to those who know you.

Odes: Appendix

Prayer of Mary the God-Bearer

My mind magnifies the Lord, and my spirit rejoices in God my savior, for he has regarded the low estate of his slave. For look, from now on all generations will call me blessed, for he who is mighty has done great things for me, and holy is his name.

His mercy is on those who fear him from generation to generation. He has shown strength with his arm, he has scattered the proud in the imagination of their hearts, he has put down the mighty from their thrones, and exalted those of low degree. He has filled the hungry with good things, and the rich he has sent away empty.

He has helped his servant Israel, in remembrance of his mercy, as he promised to our fathers, to Abraham, and to his descendants forever.

Septuagint Manuscripts

The following is a list of the Septuagint manuscripts referenced in the notes for this book.

LXX א (Codex Sinaiticus) is dated to the 4th century. Parts of it are currently located at the British Library (Add. 43725) in London, Leipzig University (Gr. 1) in Leipzig, the National Library of Russia (Gr. 2, Gr. 259, Gr. 843, Fonds. d. Ges. f. alte Lit., and Oct 156) in Saint Petersburg, and Saint Catherine's Monastery (Neus Slg. MΓ 1) on Mount Sinai.

LXX A (Codex Alexandrinus) is dated to the 5th century. It is currently located at the British Library (Royal 1 D. VIII) in London.

LXX B (Codex Vaticanus) is dated to the 4th century. It is currently located at the Vatican Library (Gr. 1209) in Vatican City.

Alternative Translations

The following is a list of alternative translations that were used for comparative analysis.

The Aleppo Codex is dated to circa 920 AD. For centuries, it was housed at the Central Synagogue of Aleppo, from which its name is derived. It was the oldest known complete copy of the Hebrew scriptures used within Judaism until 1947 when it was seized and divided among Jewish families during anti-Jewish riots in Aleppo. The sections that have resurfaced are currently at the Israel Museum in Jerusalem. Approximately 40% is still missing.

The Leningrad Codex is dated to 1008 (or 1009) AD. It is currently located at the National Library of Russia (Firkovich B 19 A) in St. Petersburg. The Leningrad Codex is the oldest complete copy of the Hebrew scriptures used within Judaism.

Genizah Manuscripts

The following is a list of the Genizah manuscripts mentioned in the notes for this book.

T-S 12.863 (Genizah manuscript A) dates to the 10th century. It is currently located at Cambridge University.

T-S 12.871 (Genizah manuscript B) dates to the 10th century. It is currently located at Cambridge University.

T-S 12.867 (Genizah manuscript C) dates to the 11th or 12th century. It is currently located at Cambridge University.

T-S AS 118.78 (Genizah manuscript D) dates to the 11th century. It is currently located at Cambridge University.

T-S AS 213.17 (Genizah manuscript F) dates to the 11th or 12th century. It is currently located at Cambridge University.

Dead Sea Scrolls

The following is a list of the Dead Sea Scrolls mentioned in the notes for this book. Most are held by the Israel Museum in Jerusalem.

DSS 1QIsaᵃ (Great Isaiah Scroll) is dated to the Herodian dynasty of Judea (37 BC to 6 AD).

DSS 4Q51 (4QSamᵃ) is dated to the Herodian dynasty of Judea (37 BC to 6 AD).

DSS 11Q5 (The Great Psalms Scroll / 11QPsᵃ) is dated to the Herodian Dynasty in Judea (37 BC to 6 AD)

DSS MUR88 (MurXII) is dated to the early Roman Period (6 to 135 AD).

Also Available

ALSO AVAILABLE

ENOCH AND METATRON SERIES:
- Books of Enoch Collection

- Secrets of Enoch

- Books of Metatron Collection

- Books of Enoch and Metatron Collection

OTHER TRANSLATIONS:
- Apocalypses of Ezra

- Arabic Maccabees

- Hebrew Maccabees

- Life of Adam and Eve

- Memories of the New Kingdom

- Septuagint's Esther and the Vetus Latina Esther

- Septuagint's Ezekiel and the Ba'al Cycle

- Septuagint's Job and the Testament of Job

- Septuagint's Proverbs and the Wisdom of Amenemope

- Syriac Maccabees – Deuterocanonical Books

- The Amarna Letters

- Testaments of the Patriarchs Collection

- Tobit and Ahikar

- Ugaritic Texts: Ba'al Cycle

- Wisdom of Ahikar